GOOD GIRL

THE FIVE FOUNDATIONS:
FROM PEOPLE-PLEASER TO POWERHOUSE

Piyané Ung

Good Girl
The Five Foundations: From people-pleaser to powerhouse
Published in 2024 by Dear Me Pty Ltd
www.piyane.com

© Piyané Ung 2024

The right of Piyané Ung to be identified as the author of this book has been asserted in accordance with the Copyright Act 1968 (Australia). No part of this publication may be reproduced, stored in a retrieval system, or transmitted, in any form or by any means, electronic, mechanic, photocopying, recording or otherwise, without the prior written permission of the publisher.

Disclaimer: The words in this book are from the life experience of the author, and in no way constitute medical or psychological advice.

National Library of Australia
Cataloguing-in-Publication entry:
ISBN: 978-1-7636780-2-6 (paperback)

A catalogue record for this book is available from the National Library of Australia

Dear Younger Piyané,
Thank you for taking me this far.
Your sacrifices, perseverance and spirit
have built me into who I am today.
This one's for you.

Contents

Are you a "good girl"?... 1

What to expect on the journey... 5

Things that are okay:
Mistakes, failings and bad days.. 18

You are your environment 25

What to know when you're in a rut... 38

Foundation 1: Physical 44

Foundation 2: Mental & emotional... 73

Foundation 3: Community 120

Foundation 4: Spiritual.. 147

Foundation 5: Financial... 174

From good girl to bad-ass woman!.. 203

"Piyané is an amazing woman, whom I am proud to claim as a dear friend. When we first met over fifteen years ago I was overwhelmed by her truly unique style, her classical elegance and grace - like she had stepped out of one of those Hollywood classic movies.

Many years later I came to recognise that she is all of that, but so much more - she is a visionary and creator who effortlessly floats the globe sharing with passion her so many talents.

Our topics of conversation are many and varied, but she is one of those people who projects through the life that she lives, that we all can and should evolve and grow and that we can do so with kindness and compassion, and share our good fortunes.

I so look forward to the release of Piyané's new book as I expect it to fascinate me by imparting a further insight in the unique "Story of Piyané" - a very dear friend and unique human."

– *Dr Tass Tasiopoulos*
M.B., B.S., B.Sc. (Hons) FCPCA

* * *

"Piyané is a good friend and role model for me. I feel very comfortable with her, which is a safe zone for me to allow myself to open up. With her powerful guidance, born from her own experience in life, she teaches me how to be strong and to continue standing up every day for myself. I'm so excited to read her book!"

– *Natacha Van, Fashion Designer*

* * *

"It is a pleasure to be able to endorse Piyané's autobiography. She visited Sunrise Orphanage in Cambodia, where we care for orphaned and abandoned children and went on to build a team of her friends to raise money for us. To the Sunrise Children it means so much to know that their fellow Cambodians want to help them. She will be a lifetime Friend of Sunrise and I know her book will inspire you."

– *Geraldine Cox (AM), Founder and Fundraising Ambassador, Sunrise Orphanage, Cambodia (www.sunrisecambodia.org.au)*

* * *

Are you a "good girl"?

Name one "good girl" who has actually achieved something she is proud of. Not something she was told or conditioned to do, but something she truly wants, just for herself.

If you're picking up this book, I'm guessing you may be going through your own journey of figuring out what you want in life. Maybe you are plagued by doubt as you are trying to pursue your own path. I get you!

But who am I to advise you? Why would I write a book like this? Am I even qualified? Do I have something worth sharing? Why would I expect you to spend time reading *my* book?

These are all the things that run through my head before I start writing this book – and even as I write it.

But that's the problem, isn't it? It's not just about this book. The same questions have plagued me in every area of my life – business, social, personal, financial. And I dare say, I'm not the only one.

For the longest time, I was a people-pleaser. If only I did this or that, my parents would be happy, and therefore I would be a good daughter. If only I made more money, then society would approve of me, and therefore I would be accepted. If I were perfect, then I would be good enough. If I didn't say "no", I would be agreeable so then I would be a "good girl". Hey, who doesn't like a good girl? We are convenient!

Good Girl

"Yes Mother, it was all my fault! Why didn't I think of that?"
"Of course Lucy, I'll drive you to your neighbour's uncle's BBQ. I'll make it work for you."
"Yes sure, schedule that meeting for midnight because you're overseas. I go to bed very late anyway."

If you can relate to this, first of all, I'm sorry. It hasn't been easy – doing so much for other people that "you" are on the bottom of your own list. At night you collapse in a heap, emotionally and physically drained – and still don't feel good enough.

From personal experience, this can go on for years, or even decades. I'm no psychologist, but I can tell you it's been the quickest and surest way to land me in a deep pit of depression.

I spent the majority of my 20s there – a hard core people-pleaser. And let me tell you, I was a very different person then. If you were to tell me then that I could run multiple businesses, travel the world and hold my own with influential people at fabulous events, or even write a book, I would have laughed at you! My self-esteem was so low, my depression had me in a headlock. I felt so utterly worthless that I hardly left the house.

So I hid behind a pretty façade on Instagram. My life looked great on the outside, but I was deeply ashamed of the person on the inside. This is where "ego" came to protect me for a period of time. Ego is often seen as a bad thing, but it's neither good nor bad. When the world perceives us in a certain way, we respond to that perception by constructing an "identity" or ego. This often happens as a result of a lack of self-awareness. As Eckhart Tolle puts it, "the ego is the unobserved mind itself."[1]

The ego is simply a tool that we use to engage with the world, until we do the deep inner work to find and develop a true sense

---

1   See Eckhart Tolle, *A New Earth: Awakening to Your Life's Purpose* (Penguin: 2005).

of self.

So the ego served me well and helped me survive for over a decade, when I didn't know who I truly was. My belief was that I wasn't good enough, I wasn't loveable, I wasn't beautiful, I wasn't smart – in short, I wasn't worthy. So the pretty pictures on Instagram compensated for all the things that I was not.

When we live in that mindset, we start chasing thing after thing, because we want validation from others. We often chase after things because we want others to see that we have them, not because we actually want these things ourselves. As a result, we end up living someone else's dream. We end up living an "avatar" that is not who we truly are.

This is why I was depressed. It is my belief that depression most often comes from not living in alignment with our true self. We believe many lies, such as not being good enough, smart enough, worthy enough, and so on. This leads us to develop an avatar which is separate from our true self. The longer we live in these false beliefs, the deeper the split between this avatar and the vision of our true self.

The first step to becoming our true self is to recognise the split. The even bigger challenge is learning to pivot from the avatar to the powerhouse that we truly are. This is the work of a lifetime – I'm certainly still working on it.

So this book is about how I have pivoted towards my higher self, and still continue to do so.

But aren't you still living a pretty façade, Piyané?

Yes, 100%!

We don't live in the Stone Age. People often don't ask for your phone number anymore – they ask for your Instagram. My Instagram is now my "resumé".

Good Girl

I work in fashion and one of my primary businesses is a skincare company. It makes sense that I have a social media presence in this area. Yes, it's still a façade, to a certain degree – because I only show you what I want to show you.

The old façade served the purpose of hiding my insecurities and shame. It was driven by fear and therefore the need for validation.

Now, my social media is intentional and strategic. It is a resumé for potential investors, business partners and clients. Most importantly, it serves a different purpose – it serves my community by sharing my authentic self and the insights I've gained through my self-development, insights that are aligned with my higher self. I filter what I share based on my choices, rather than censoring what I post based on the opinions of others. My social media now serves me and others, rather than serving my need for validation.

What to expect on the journey

I don't claim to have it all together – and I'm okay with that. In this book, I'm happy to share with you what has got me out of the pit of depression, but I'm still figuring things out. My aim is to be authentic with you about my journey along the way.

I don't want to be happy all the time. Happiness is just a fleeting emotion, like anger or excitement. Rather, I seek to be authentically content. I recognise that there's still a long way for me to go, but I no longer criticise myself for my failings and struggles. This means I can accept my bad days and know that, along with the good, they are shaping me for the better, and my life is more fulfilled as a result. I don't despair at the bad days and I don't gloat at the good ones, because I know that both "good" and "bad" are temporary.

Do you know how I know this? One of my hobbies is collecting written postcards from decades ago, some even dating back to the 1920s. The ones I've collected from Europe are in different languages, so I never used to understand what they said. Now, with thanks to Artificial Intelligence, even the faded, almost illegible handwriting has been translated. And just like that, I have a sneak peek into people's lives, hopes, fears, regrets and loves. One hundred years later, these people are no longer alive, but their words live on and are tangible in my hands. How privileged am I to glimpse this!

Good Girl

It also makes me realise that everything in life is temporary. The big celebrations and heartbreaks these people experienced are long gone. Eventually, just like them, I will be gone too – and with me, my celebrations and heartbreaks. Someone might read this book in years to come and also ponder my life, just as I ponder the lives of these people from the past.

In this book I will share some personal traumatic experiences. In doing so, I am hoping to show you how I have turned my scars into art – for me. I have debated whether to include some of these personal stories, but ultimately the purpose of this book is to inspire you to find your voice and own your own stories, so that you may also turn your scars into art – for you.

That said, you and I are different. My good days and your good days might not look the same; equally, my bad days and your bad days might differ.

You might scroll through my Instagram account and see me glammed up in ballgowns and jewels, or posing on ski slopes, or glowing with pride at a Nalia Cosmetics launch. You may make the assumption that my life is perfect and I've always been confident and successful. Believe me, the truth is *very* different. As you read my stories – some recent, others from the distant past – I hope you can see that for yourself.

If everybody likes you, you don't like yourself

Let's start with a disclaimer, and it might sound shocking: following the ideas in this book will make people dislike you. Not everyone, not the people who matter in the grand scheme of things, but some people.

Why? Because, by working through the teachings and tools in this book and applying them to your life, you will undergo change. And some people will dislike this new, improved you.

What to expect on the journey

It's understandable: from their perspective you're no longer the compliant, sweet, self-sacrificing person you always were. Suddenly you aren't the "nice girl" who automatically says "yes" when people ask her to perform tasks for them. Suddenly you're no longer the "good" friend who always defers her needs to avoid upsetting others, or the "good" co-worker who absorbs mountains of extra work without complaint, or the "good" mother who lets her child walk all over her.

Now you have boundaries. You have a clear sense of what matters to you, you're working at prioritising your needs over those of others, and you say "no" when you want to or need to. You're no longer a people-pleaser, and some of those people you used to please will dislike that.

Others may be surprised at first, and then adapt to you, respecting that you've matured and changed.

Some will despise it and might even stop being in your life altogether because this new boundary doesn't serve them. Well, that's okay too.

I want to tell you something important I've learned on my journey. *It's okay not to be liked.* It's okay to be the bad guy in other people's stories. You are not for everybody. If everybody likes you, it probably means you don't like yourself enough to set boundaries with others; it probably means you consistently put their needs before yours. If you like yourself, you have clear boundaries – and some people won't like that because you're not easily manipulated or used.

So, while you're working through this book, don't be alarmed if you start losing friends and family members. It's part of the process. Because you only have 24 hours in a day, you don't have time for everybody. And if some people take it personally and don't understand that you need to prioritise yourself, possibly

Good Girl

"disappearing" at times to take care of your needs, they are not your people.

Are you a people-pleaser? Here are some common symptoms:

- Apologising for things for which you aren't responsible
- Avoiding conflict
- Worrying unduly about people's reactions
- Struggling to say "no" when others ask you to do things for them
- Changing personality according to who you're with
- Looking to others for your self-worth: feeling good about yourself when you get praise and validation and losing confidence when you don't

People-pleasers feel responsible for other people's emotions and will contort themselves into all sorts of uncomfortable positions to keep others happy – at great personal cost. I know because I used to be one. You run around like a headless chicken trying to make everyone happy: you need to make sure your daughter's happy, your son's happy, your husband's happy, your parents have everything they need, your in-laws love you, your co-workers think you're great. Plus, you've got to keep those dishes sparkling, the laundry clean and folded and meals prepared. Eventually, you collapse from exhaustion. Because you've been so busy taking care of others, your own physical, mental and spiritual health have gone out the window. "Good girls" end up running themselves into the ground.

If you are a people-pleaser, you're never good enough, no matter what you do. If this describes you, please don't be too harsh on yourself. As a reformed people-pleaser myself, I understand. I didn't start off as a confident young woman; I'm 36 and it took

What to expect on the journey

me quite a few years to become one. To get to this version of me, several previous versions of Piyané had to die, and plenty of habits and ways of thinking had to fall by the wayside. Our brains are computers, calculating on our behalf every moment of the day without us even being aware of it. The problem is that we keep functioning on old programs – and if we keep doing the same thing, we'll keep getting the same result.

How do you tune into what you want and need? How do you avoid getting used by other people? By listening to your gut. The problem, as I discovered, is that when we're depressed we can't hear what our gut is telling us. Our head might be telling us things like, "This world is not safe. It's best not to be a part of it". Believe me, I know how hard it is to trust yourself when you have terrifying thoughts like these projecting themselves onto you. That's why the first task is to get yourself into a better state, step by step. The Five Foundations will help you craft a healthy lifestyle that will support you when things are going well, as well as when they're not.

Here's something else you need to know: this book will not magically heal you. You won't read it and suddenly feel better. It isn't a magic pill that will fix your problems overnight or transform your life in a day, even though you might be saying, "Yup, give me the Five Foundations; that's what I'm going to do all day tomorrow." Guess what? Life will inevitably get in the way!

I've been on this journey for six years and I've found that I go up and down, up and down, again and again. It's life. During the up times, I might be on the go for a solid three months, waking up with a smile, excited about the day ahead, practising self-love and meditation, going to the gym regularly, feeling good in my body, showing up for all the meetings I must attend and generally holding everything together.

Good Girl

Then there will be months when everything is erratic: I might be travelling a lot, not exercising as much as I should, not prioritising myself sufficiently because there are just too many things to do in one day. I might get sick or my daughter might get sick, and then I start thinking, "Gee, my businesses aren't going too well." Then one of my product launches gets pushed back and expenses start mounting and there's no income, and life becomes stressful. And because I post about fashion and skincare on my Instagram, they now call me an "influencer". At first I didn't even know what that meant, but I do know that part of having a social media presence is keeping up appearances; after all, it's part of my business, part of my job – I have to attend events, pose for photos, film and edit content, add captions, and post online. Look, I'm not complaining – it's been a privilege to be an "influencer" – but amid all this, my personal needs sometimes slip down to the bottom of the list again. So a structure, a system must be in place so my life can have balance.

That's when I need to return to the Five Foundations. In fact, as I'm writing this book, it's reminding me to practise these habits again.

Here is where I must make another disclaimer. During my deep pit of depression, I took myself to therapy, hired a life coach, attended many seminars online and in person, and read any self-development books I could find. But as my journey progressed, my "recovery" was still up and down, and I found myself going back and forth between therapy, life coaches and these hundreds of books. I got confused about which advice to follow. I pushed on and got myself out of one rut after another. After a while I noticed the dip would not be as deep, and I wouldn't stay there as long. I used to spend months in a depressive state, then weeks, then just days. Eventually I found myself catching sight

What to expect on the journey

of the "symptoms", the tell-tale signs of another looming dip approaching. Without even knowing it at the time, I started to practise the Five Foundations, that I am now spelling out for you.

I journal a lot, which is something I learned from my coach. At first I found it very hard to write my thoughts down because I didn't even know where to begin, but most importantly I was scared that someone might read it. Remember, I grew up in a very conservative and poor family, where privacy was a luxury. My parents love me very much. In an attempt to protect me, especially in my teenage years, they saw fit to go through my things regularly to make sure I wasn't hiding anything "stupid" such as a love-note. So I avoided journalling for 30 years. The first few times I started journalling, at the age of 30, I found it a huge struggle. I wrote random things, mostly nice comments. I was still scared that someone might find and read my journal. But, as they say, "practice makes perfect". With the help and guidance of my coach at the time, I finally claimed the pages I journalled as my own, and found that the words that came out were natural and courageous. My coach taught me that my life is mine. My time is mine. And the pages were mine.

"Piyané, when are you going to claim it?"

So I became more and more emboldened and honest in my journals. From angry words, to excited words, to dreams and fantasies. I've been taught by Tony Robbins, a renowned philanthropist and coach: Don't reinvent the wheel, just model someone successful.[2] So I've learned many things from the hundreds of books I've read. At 33 years of age, depending on the month and the books that I was reading at the time, you might catch me talking about a range of things that inspired me,

---

2 See the official website of Tony Robbins for more information: www.tonyrobbins.com.

Good Girl

and the actions I followed from the books' instructions. One book taught me how to build habits (*Atomic Habits*[3]), one book taught me about the wisdom of life itself (*The Four Agreements*[4]), and another taught me how to have confidence in myself (*You are a Badass*[5]). These are a few books I read, but when I was in crisis or felt self-doubt, sadness, grief, or like I had failed, I found myself scrambling through these pages to find exactly what to do – not just words of encouragement, but a clear structure with tiny actions for me to take to avoid falling into a dip again. I hardly ever found this kind of clear guidance. Just like watching Netflix, you often end up spending more time scrolling to find the perfect movie to watch than actually watching the movie itself.

Finally, one day, during fourteen days of quarantine in an Australian hotel after travelling from Cambodia during the COVID Pandemic, I had nowhere to go and words just poured out. This time it was different. For the first time ever, I mapped out my life, including a list of Foundations to help me function. I said to myself, "OK Piyané, with all of the hundreds of books you have read, what are the takeaway messages?" The list was long and I meditated on all the things that mattered to my life.

I have shortened these insights down to Five Foundations. Finally, I can understand why my life always felt up and down and the reasons I kept returning to all my books and studies to find the perfect tool to get back on track, still failing to choose which

---

3   James Clear, *Atomic Habits: An Easy & Proven Way to Build Good Habits & Break Bad Ones* (Penguin: 2018).

4   Don Miguel Ruiz, *The Four Agreements: A Practical Guide to Personal Freedom* (Amber-Allen Publishing: 1997).

5   Jen Sincero, *You are a Badass: How to Stop Doubting Your Greatness and Start Living an Awesome Life* (Running Press: 2013).

What to expect on the journey

technique to adopt. I looked at my hand-written scribblings and the charts in my journals and realised these five things are most fundamental in my life:

1. **My physical health.** Without this, I wouldn't have the energy to do or accomplish anything.
2. **My mental and emotional wellbeing.** Without this, I would feel like crap and nothing else would be possible.
3. **My spiritual wellbeing.** I'm not your typical religious type but I must have faith – in myself, in others, and especially in the force that created me and the events around me. Because, *my God*, imagine if things happened in order just to happen. I would forever be a victim!
4. **My community.** I can't do anything worthwhile alone. I need genuine support systems, people I can call at 3 a.m. just to cry. People who can give me counsel and vice versa. People I can call to share my good news, without them being jealous – or my bad news, without them secretly celebrating it or putting me down. When I become successful, I will share the wealth with my community and loved ones – because, otherwise, what's the point?
5. **My finances.** Being completely honest here, whilst money might not directly buy us happiness, it sure can do a lot of things!

So once I put the Foundations in place, the next part was easy. During the last few days of my quarantine, I started writing down actions, small actions I could do everyday to take care of, and foster, these Five Foundations – to make each one stronger. I realised I had failed in the past because in all the books I read I practised just part of the "Foundations". For example, in the

Good Girl

month when I read *Can't Hurt Me* by David Goggins,[6] I went to the gym constantly and neglected the other four Foundations. Though I felt good physically, my life did not move forward in ways I wanted it to. In the month that I read *Dare to Lead* by Brené Brown,[7] I started to have the courage to be more authentically vulnerable in my sphere of work, but I stopped going to the gym.

With these Five Foundations, I have made it as easy as I can, so that I can practise them everyday. I broke them down into small actions that I could do everyday and, from the skills I learned from *Atomic Habits*, I started building my own small structure.

Three years later, at the age of 36, when I'm about to go into a dip, without fail I have realised that one of the Foundations must be in a weakened state. Then I go back to basics and practise the Five Foundations. And it works – time and time again!

So now I am gifting these Five Foundations to you because, what the hell... if it works for me, it might work for you too. And hey, if it doesn't, what do you have to lose trying?

This book is my holy grail: a collection of all the tools I have practised repeatedly to get myself well, then stopped and re-started, multiple times. When life gets in the way, you shift priorities and, before you know it, you're in a rut again. So, expect to find times when you'll need to start over from the beginning. But please know that the next time you're in a rut, the dip will not be as deep, and you won't stay down there as long. And you'll have these guidelines to get you back on track. It's an up and down journey – in the right direction.

---

6   David Goggins, *Can't Hurt Me: Master Your Mind and Defy the Odds* (Lioncrest Publishing: 2018).

7   Brené Brown, *Dare to Lead: Brave Work. Tough Conversations. Whole Hearts* (Random House: 2018).

What to expect on the journey

Whenever you feel the need, return to this book and re-read it or re-listen to it. The journey isn't smooth; it has stops and starts, and sometimes you will take a couple of steps backward before you go forward again. Don't be too hard on yourself if you slip back to the way you were and become depressed again. It's okay: just pick up the book and start again. If you have been to therapy and then stopped, it's okay to make another appointment. Hire a coach if you feel the need. But know that this time around, you aren't starting from scratch. This time you're re-starting with experience.

This brings me to an important point: don't try to take on too much at once. Change shouldn't be overwhelming, because when we make drastic changes, we're unlikely to continue on the path. I don't want you using the tools for a week and then thinking, "Argh! This is too much!" My suggestion is to start slowly, just a few minutes of the Five Foundations every day. That's all – just five minutes; keep it manageable. Sticking to that will build your self-respect, which is the key ingredient in your confidence.

Think of it this way: if we take a long flight and we go just slightly off-course from our city of departure, we will find ourselves at an entirely different destination when we land. Deviate minutely and we'll probably end up in Antarctica, not Australia! Similarly, whatever small changes we make in our lives will help take us to a different place the next time we go through a dip – a better place. It's worth doing the work, because even a tiny bit, done regularly, can change the outcome.

What this book can do for you

When you decide to embark on a personal journey, things start to shift. Here are some of the ways this book may benefit you:

- **Provide you with a solid structure for living.** We all need structure and guidance in our lives. The Five Foundations are there to support you as you make your way in life, in both good times and bad. We need structure when we are feeling overwhelmed – when we have family to take care of, as well as facing issues with our partner, children, parents or work. Perhaps there are also pressures like health or financial problems. The Five Foundations are tools to help nurture your body, your mind, your emotions, your spiritual side (even though you might not think you have one) and your money.
- **Help you create a circle of support.** If you start to use the tools, you will develop the support network you need to pull you through hard times. You won't be doing life by yourself any more. To me, Foundation 3, which is about community and our connection with others, is the most important. When everything else has gone to pieces (our physical and mental well-being, our sense of purpose), it's our relationships that are crucial. They are what will keep us going until the rough patch has passed.

Keep working this book and you will cultivate friends who are there for you. I'll share tips and tools to help you find and nurture those relationships. The truth is that some people don't have friends: now that many of us are living such insular lives, no longer with our extended family, it can be hard to make friends – especially in our 30s, 40s and 50s, when many of us are busy, working parents. People's lives are full to the brim with their kids, partners, businesses – they don't often have time for coffee and a catch-up! When I was 30 I didn't have any friends, but there are ways to make friends and I will teach you how. I

What to expect on the journey

now have a group of trusted people who will come to my aid at 3 a.m.; I know I can count on them, and I will show up and do the same for each of them. Authentic, long-lasting relationships are vital: when life takes a dive (and at times it will), you have these people to remind you of who you are.

- **Show you how to build confidence.** Self-respect builds confidence. If you keep your word, you will have self-respect – and nobody else needs to know about it. It's easy to keep your word to others, because other people hold you accountable – but what we'll work on is keeping your word towards *yourself*. Nobody else needs to know what you've promised to yourself, but keeping your word to yourself helps you become a person of integrity. Over time you will know that even in difficult situations you'll be able to prioritise your needs instead of putting them aside to avoid inconveniencing someone else. That kind of trust in yourself gives you confidence.
- **Help you align your life with your values.** Sometimes it's hard to know who we are and what we really want from life under all the layers of conditioning and people-pleasing. Once we find out what our true values and desires are, we can start aligning our actions with them.
- **Show you how to accept failure and rough patches as a part of life.** These things are natural and inevitable. Work the tools, and next time the dip won't be as bad.

Things that are okay: Mistakes, failings and bad days

Ten years ago, I was a vastly different person. I thought I was just good to look at, and even though inside I knew I was smart, I hid it. I'd often doubt myself and think I wasn't smart enough to be in business.

Many things have happened in my life that I'm not proud of; decisions I've made that I later regretted. Back then, I associated those experiences with shame. I want you to know that *shame* is a powerful word. When we screw up, we often feel embarrassed about it. If we honestly admit that we made a mistake – "What I *did* was wrong" – that relates to the actions we took. But when we feel shame, we associate feeling bad with who we are as people. Then shame isn't about what we did anymore but who we *are*. And that isn't a helpful way of thinking for a happy, successful life.

Today, I'm not ashamed of the mistakes I've made. Shame is the quickest way to lose self-esteem, self-respect and the value we place on ourselves. If you're prone to feelings of embarrassment and shame when you've made a mistake, please hear me say that *you are being too hard on yourself*.

Failings show us that we tried, we stuck our necks out and did something, which is a whole lot better than being too afraid to try something new. Progress all comes back to us making better decisions every day. And sometimes we will all fail. Let me make

Things that are okay

that clear from the get-go, we will fail many, many, *many* times. Making mistakes along the way is how we learn and grow. A lot of internal changes take place after failing at several businesses, believe me! I've learned many things on my journey, and one of the key lessons is this: never call *yourself* a failure. The failings you've experienced are just stepping stones to better things.

If I tell myself I'm a failure because a business I started has folded, will I approach the CEO who has just stepped into the room to ask him if he's interested in investing in my new business? Probably not. When our self-esteem is low, we pass over opportunities in life. But when we believe we are worthy, we take opportunities that present themselves – and our world opens up. Play the hand you're dealt in life as if it's the hand you've chosen, and you will never lose. You can't control external factors like your environment, your parents or your work, but you can control yourself and how you think – and if I can change my thinking, you can too.

I have failed at more than 30 businesses since I was eighteen, but if I'd stopped after the last one failed, I wouldn't have the thriving businesses I have today. Even so, some of my businesses are successful and some aren't. It's okay to make mistakes: you learn from your experiences, you pick yourself up and you keep going. Success is about the will to keep on going. It's also about *why* you keep going. What are you doing all this for? Many people don't have a vision – and if that's you, it's okay. It's especially hard to envisage your future when you're depressed or going through a hard time.

Where I am now is a place that I'd call "happily imperfect". I could tell you my life is fabulous every day, but that's not the case. My life isn't perfect, but I can honestly say that I am content. Not 100 percent happy with everything I've got – but I know I'm working

Good Girl

towards something I love, and that sense of purpose brings me fulfilment. Besides, I'm not aiming for perfection; nobody has a good day every day. I'm not striving to wake up with butterflies flitting round my head and birds singing and rats running errands for me like Cinderella. The secret to contentment for me, every single day, is paying attention to the Five Foundations. They allow me to accept that bad days are okay. And I'm not ashamed of my bad days.

Right now, even as I'm writing this book, I'm in what I would call an "erratic state". This is one of those times when life has got in the way. I'm a bit stressed and my routine is out of whack. I'm not in my "winning streak"; life is not flowing smoothly and predictably and I'm not feeling on top of things.

This is how my "erratic" day went today. This morning I woke up at 9 a.m. because I went to sleep very late last night. I'm usually in bed at a reasonable hour, but last night I couldn't sleep because I was stressed. My eight-year-old daughter has been ill this past week and I had to take her to hospital for treatment. Also, my business is going through a rough patch, plus there are issues in my personal life and a bunch of other worries. All this put me in a stressed state of mind and I wasn't able to tune out and sleep. I went to bed at 2.30 or 3 a.m. and woke up feeling really fatigued six hours later.

I'm writing this from Cambodia, as I'm based in both Phnom Penh and Melbourne. My businesses are mostly in Australia, so when I woke up here this morning it was already 1 p.m. in Australia – which meant I already had 50 emails waiting and had to play catch-up. I spent an hour in bed, replying to the messages and responding to employees, contractors and suppliers. I was feeling rather scattered and overwhelmed, but because I have all the resources, tips and tools I'm going to outline in this book, I could

Things that are okay

stay centred throughout the rest of the day.

From 10 to 11 a.m. I had a meeting. Then I got ready for lunch with a friend at 11.30. You have to maintain your networks, and I always try to make time for these relationships, even when my schedule is tight. Lunch finished at 1.30, and from 2 to 3.30 p.m. I had another meeting, before going to pick up my daughter after choir practice at 4 p.m. followed by another meeting for an hour and a half. Later I got ready for dinner with friends from High School; again, your network is your net worth (as Tony Robbins says).

Throughout the day I checked my WhatsApp, my Slack, my emails and responded to messages wherever possible – because my assistant recently left the job and I haven't yet found a replacement for her.

I want to emphasise that I can't do everything myself. I delegate as much as possible, and that wasn't always the case. Perhaps you are embarking on your entrepreneurial journey or your path out of people-pleasing. You might not have the capacity yet to ask for help or to delegate tasks to others but, as time goes on, as you read this book and start to apply all the tools, you will learn to delegate. For those tasks that aren't particularly in your strongest skillset – which someone else could do just as well as you, or even better – consider handing them over. You will learn to value your time more, because as you progress in your journey – emotionally, mentally, and especially financially – you will realise that your time is the most valuable resource you could ever have.

Something I realise is that if I didn't have the resources and tools I have today, I would be in a rut right now, for weeks if not months. Being a reformed people-pleaser, when stresses hit, I tend to default to pleasing others and not wanting to disappoint anyone. At this very moment, I can say a) yes, I'm in an erratic state, and b) I'm still happy, content and grounded.

I'm proud of that.

The aim isn't to eradicate stress from our lives altogether. Newsflash: it doesn't matter where you go or what you do, you will always be met with problems and obstacles. The grass isn't greener on the other side. The key is finding problems you enjoy solving, and little ways to find contentment and fulfilment alongside the stress. It's important to find and nurture the *resources* to better deal with stress, pressure and difficult situations, and not to resort to feelings of shame, embarrassment and unworthiness when things don't go as planned.

Your attitude towards life is what makes for a good day.

For me, a good day starts with getting a solid eight hours of sleep, so I can go out feeling refreshed. It's not necessarily about waking up feeling I can take on the world and everything being Hollywood-movie perfect; a good day is simply when I feel content and happy in myself.

When I wake up, the first thing I do is switch on my phone, but it's not to scroll mindlessly through social media. What I do is check my calendar to remind myself of what I have on that day; this gives me clarity and peace of mind. Then I get up, have breakfast, brush my teeth and do stretches.

A good day means starting my morning slowly and having the freedom to spend my time however I want. Nowadays, I choose when to have my coffee, and when to have my meetings. If I'm not feeling well, I reschedule arrangements. To me, this is the ideal: being able to take care of myself and my family, spend time with loved ones if I want to – and, if a business opportunity pops up at 2 p.m., having the freedom to pursue it.

A good day can mean waking up and having eight hours

Things that are okay

of work ahead of me, knowing that there are many families I'm feeding under my employment. A good day for me means knowing my employees will go home also having had a good day because I showed up and did my job well. I feel pleased knowing that they have secure jobs, are paid well and can put food on their table. On another day I might be attending Fashion Week where I meet inspirational people in bizarre outfits who somehow capture the essence of a beautiful dream, and I walk away thinking, "Wow, that challenged my limited way of looking at the world."

I'll admit it, I do have a lot of amazing days. I might wake up overlooking the beach, work for an hour or two, then take a leisurely walk along the shore. After breakfast, I'll have a swim and a scuba dive, then come back and check a few emails and, after lunch, have an afternoon nap. Later, I'll take my time getting ready for dinner. I adore putting on makeup and it's a joy to have the time to do it. This is something I do to please myself, not anyone else; it's therapeutic for me, like painting.

A good day can come in many forms. For this lifestyle, there are five things I need to ensure I have in place, namely:

- physical fitness
- mentally & emotionally nourishment
- financially security
- connection with others, and
- faith in something greater than myself

All these elements support me and allow me to have a good day. Most importantly, though, it's the *emotion* I am feeling that turns a day into a good one, because it's possible to wake up in a penthouse with a beautiful view and feel completely indifferent

Good Girl

to it. Six years ago, when I was 30 and what I can confidently say was in the depths of my depression, I would wake up in my 41st floor city apartment and my first thought wasn't, "Oh, what a gorgeous view!" Rather, my first thought was, "I should jump off this balcony."

So, you could say, I've learned this the hard way: it doesn't matter where you are or how beautiful the view is – if you feel trapped in your life, and like your time isn't yours, then your life isn't yours, then everything is going to feel pointless. Your attitude towards life is what makes for a good day. And that is something we will work on together.

You are your environment

To understand my journey, you need to know a bit about my background. Let me take you back into the past and tell you some of where I have come from.

I'm half-Cambodian, half-Chinese; my mother is pure Chinese and my father is pure Cambodian. Growing up in Cambodia, I never felt I fitted in. This might not sound like a big deal because there are so many Chinese in Cambodia, but back then, Chinese people were considered somewhat more elite than the Cambodian people. Chinese were whiter, for starters, and both Cambodian and Chinese people prefer pale skin. My skin is not white; it's a gorgeous honey colour, I now realise – people try to get skin like this from tanning! But while I was growing up I hated my skin. I wanted to be whiter, because that's what everybody liked. People would often say to me, "Oh, your mother's so white. Why are you so black?" and I would have no answer for them.

I have an older sister and we grew up without much. I didn't know it at the time, but looking back I can see that we weren't well off by any means. My parents are beautiful people and they did everything they could to raise us in a good environment, but they both grew up in extremely difficult and traumatic circumstances: both my mother and father survived the Khmer Rouge. This was the radical Communist movement that ruled Cambodia from 1975 to 1979, after coming to power through a

Good Girl

guerrilla war. The Khmer Rouge forcibly evacuated the major cities, making millions of people leave their homes and relocate to communal farms and rural camps. The Khmer Rouge was on a mission to create a peasant utopia, a classless society where people worked the land and were self-sufficient. Unfortunately, this vision caused untold suffering. Led by dictator Pol Pot, the regime was brutal and led to the genocide of Cambodian people: it's estimated that between 1.6 million and 2 million civilians were killed by starvation, torture, execution, medical experiments, lack of medicines, forced marches, forced labour and other kinds of violence. It's hard to imagine but a quarter of the Cambodian population was killed during that time.

My mother had nine siblings and only four of them survived. Both her parents were either slaughtered or starved to death during the Khmer regime. I don't know much about my father's side of the family, but I do know his parents were murdered too.

So, these two "broken" people met, fell in love, married, and did their best to raise my sister and me, but naturally they had their own issues, having witnessed such violence and acts of inhumanity.

I know a tragic story about my mother and grandmother in the camps. There, children were kept separate from their mothers, in tents with other kids in their age group. My mother was eleven years old at the time and her group had their own camp, far away from all the other age cohorts. People were housed in the camps according to their purpose: those in their 30s would be working the fields or carving wooden items out in the sun, for example.

Everyone was given very small portions of food and this was very deliberate: if you aren't fed well, you don't have the energy to fight back, so the people were starved over time and kept weak. My mother would always save some of her food to give to

You are your environment

her mother. Picture her every night, sneaking out of the children's tent, which was situated far from her mother's tent, to take her mother a bit of food and make sure she was alright.

One night when she was about thirteen, as usual my mother raced to the adults' tent, but her mother wasn't there. She discovered that her mother had died. Can you imagine how devastated this little girl would have been? I have an eight-year-old daughter which makes this story even more heartbreaking for me.

Because of their experiences, I have full compassion for my parents.

It doesn't make what happened to me okay, though. For example, I'd always feel ashamed when my parents fed me something nice, because they'd invariably say things like, "You have it easy. When I was your age, I was eating starvation rations and working all day." That meant I never felt I was enough while growing up. How could I compare myself with my parents? How could I complain? If I made mistakes and got punished, my parents would say, "Stop crying! Why are you crying? Do you know, when I was younger, X and Y happened?" Or when I was experiencing some hardship, I'd complain to my mother. She would first show me compassion and love, but then she'd say, "You know, back in the day, X and Y happened to me." I was never validated, and my problems were never enough. In their eyes I didn't have any "real" problems.

Now that I'm older, I realise that someone is just as drowned at 10 feet as they are at 100 feet. It doesn't matter if your trauma was that your mother died when you were thirteen, or that your father beat you to a pulp when you were fifteen. Either way, you can fall into the same kind of hole, feeling you aren't good enough and that life isn't worth living.

Good Girl

I say this with all the love for my father, and I don't think he would even realise it, but I was afraid of him while I was growing up, especially in my teenage years. Later in the book I describe a specific experience that affected me deeply. It broke me in a way, and it took me a decade and a half to recover from it.

When you grow up in an environment where you are afraid of your parents, you learn to "read the room", and adjust your behaviour accordingly.

When I was growing up, I didn't receive love unconditionally, so I had to try to earn my parents' love and approval by being a enough of a "good girl". Everything had to be good enough: grades, outfits, hair, behaviour, even the way I spoke, dished up my food, sat down or ate.

And even then, I was never good enough. There was always something I could have done to improve. There was always something I was criticised about.

As Lauren Eden puts it, "When you are not fed love on a silver spoon you learn to lick it off knives."

Keep in mind, my parents were both very loving – they just didn't know how to express their love in a healthy way. They were scared I would be "spoiled" if they gave me positive reinforcement. However, I know that they were criticised heavily themselves growing up, and all of their actions towards me came from a good place. They were trying to prepare me for the harsh realities of adult life which they had faced and knew I needed to be equipped for. They really did try their best to love me, in ways that they thought would benefit me.

When I was younger, my father was my hero. We were a poor household with one small TV, but we had satellite for $10 a month, which was rare for our neighbourhood. Through this I was exposed to a fabulous variety of TV shows: we had MTV and

You are your environment

Cartoon Network, for example. This was my window into the big wide world, and I loved it.

One day, when I was about ten, I saw some white kids in America eating a huge tub of ice cream on TV, and I thought, "I *really* want to eat that." Then a supermarket opened across the road; before, there had only been wet markets, not supermarkets, and my father went to the new shop and bought ice cream for me. I sat eating this big tub of ice cream while watching a movie on TV and it was the best thing ever. He would smile and we were so happy. This was the most glamorous thing I'd ever experienced in my life! My father was my hero; he would get me everything I wanted.

Puberty hit me a bit earlier than other girls. I was always a tall kid, slender with big hips, and I was sexualised early by the people in our community. Cambodian people are very straightforward: they'll make comments like "Oh, you're fat", or "Hey, you're black". They'd say to me, "Oh, you're beautiful" or "You have nice hips" or "Man, you're tall!" And by the time I was thirteen, my father was starting to see me as a woman and no longer as his little child. That's when he began putting a whole lot of expectations on me: suddenly I couldn't be playful anymore. I had to chew with my mouth closed now – even though he'd tell me this while chewing with his own mouth open! I couldn't understand this change because I was Daddy's little girl. He would rub my back when I was little before I go to bed, and sometimes even sing to me. Then suddenly he just distanced himself, and he started treating me like a rebel. From the age of thirteen, like any other teenager, I started to have friends and develop my own personality. None of it met with his approval. I was under constant scrutiny – I wasn't even allowed to watch sports anymore.

Growing up, I didn't have the freedom to speak my mind and

Good Girl

do the things I wanted to do, which is why I believe today that freedom is the ultimate form of wealth. You can have all the money in the world, but if you're working sixteen hours a day, isn't that still poverty? If you're happy doing that, fine – but I'm not! To me, wealth is being free to do whatever I want: to say whatever I want to; to smile, to laugh loudly, even to chew with my mouth open if I feel like it.

Something important to point out is that I feel my story didn't happen *to* me, but *for* me. Yes, my experiences led me to feel depressed about my life – particularly the punishment meted out by my father when I was fifteen, which I will explain later on. But now I'm older and wiser, I have been through hundred of hours of therapy over the last six years, and I have a team comprising of two therapists and a coach, who help me to function mentally at the level I do today.

I have reached a state of acceptance. Those things happened and they made me resilient: I don't bend under pressure, for example. They also made me compassionate: I know that bad things happen and I have empathy for others because bad things happened to me too. I now have a higher purpose, which is why I wanted to write this book: to share my voice with you, and to inspire you to share your voice. If I hadn't had those experiences, I might not give a toss about helping other people. I'd just be drinking my martini and having a nice life! Because of my past traumas, I now want to make a difference to others. I'm the person I am today *because* of these experiences, both good and bad, and everything that happened brought me here.

Start a business because you want to build a better future.

I haven't worked for anybody since I was eighteen years old, which means I've worked for myself for half my life. I've always

You are your environment

had an aversion to authority, probably because the authority figures in my life were not the most positive influences; in fact, I feel they abused their authority over me.

I've started many businesses – from a clothing line to a music promotion business to a crêpe outlet – and many of them failed. For example, I visited Japan with a close relative (who is also a dear friend), and ate a delicious crêpe. We thought crêpes like this would take off in Cambodia, so we invested in a franchise, which wasn't successful. I spent a whole month in Tokyo seeing nothing but crêpe pans and sacks of flour! One whole month, then it failed anyway.

Along the way, however, I've had some successes. Hey, at least now I can make crêpes for you if you ever come to dinner! A while back, I had had enough of businesses, so I enrolled in an airline cadetship. Yes, I can fly. Don't be too excited for me though. I can only fly a small plane with a single engine and single instrument. I quickly realised it wasn't for me. I like creativity, and flying to the same destination everyday isn't for me.

When I was younger, I had a driving need to make money and become rich. While I was growing up, my parents always said they wanted me to go to university after school. My father comes from a long line of educators – his grandfather was a school principal – so he'd always envisaged me getting a professional qualification: to become a doctor, a lawyer, an accountant or an engineer, for example, because you get paid well in these professions. I love my parents, but growing up I felt "less than...", often wondering whether my father had wanted a son instead of a daughter after my elder sister had been born. Still, he had expectations of me being academically successful. My parents wanted to give me a good start in life and an education, because they'd never had the opportunity themselves, both having gone

Good Girl

through the Khmer Rouge. I am so grateful for all the opportunities that they have given me, although at the time I resented it. I secretly despise the expectations they placed on me because I didn't think they wanted me to succeed; they just wanted me to have fancy degrees so they could show me off like a show-pony at family BBQs! They wanted to ensure I wasn't looked down on as uneducated. However, the other people in my life, my aunties and so forth, never really agreed with women going to school.

One day, when I was fourteen, this fact hit me. Our family home was right next to the wet market, and my parents used to rent out part of the front of our house to traders and vendors. In Cambodia, there's a free and vibrant entrepreneur mentality: you don't encounter all the regulations you do in the US or Australia, for example, where you need a permit even to sell lemonade. In Cambodia you can pretty much sell whatever you want. So, my mother was renting out part of our house to a tailor, a friend of the family who made traditional Cambodian dresses and other such garments. At school the girls were taught to sew (whilst the boys did workshop), and I thought, "Oh, this will be a fun project!" I was interested in making a pair of shorts from some cool fabric I'd seen, so I'd come home from school, sit with the tailors and work on my sewing project.

One afternoon while I was cutting the fabric, a close relative came to visit. She said, "Yeah, that's good, Piyané, you're learning to sew, learning to do all these useful things." She turned to my mother and asked, "Why isn't she doing this more? Why are you letting her go to school? She shouldn't be going to school. It's impractical. She's going to be getting married anyway, and what are you going to do then with that piece of paper from school?"

I thought, *Wow*.

Thankfully, my parents always prioritised my education.

You are your environment

I'm blessed that they wanted me to finish school, for whatever reason. But here's another issue. Although my parents wanted me to have an education, there was always the idea while I was growing up that I should marry someone rich – someone to fund me – so I could be a housewife.

Looking back, I realise I grew up in a conflicted space. My upbringing conditioned me to be successful but not too successful. It was considered ideal to be pretty but not too pretty, because then you'd be intimidating to other women. Be sexy but not too sexy, because then you were slutty. Be smart, but not too smart, or you'd intimidate men. Essentially, the message was "be good at things – but not too good."

It's hardly surprising that at times women feel anxious, depressed and confused. To be who I am today, I had to "unlearn" a lot of my conditioning and change my belief systems. I'd been running on a program that no longer reflected my values; the "housewife" program didn't align with what I believed or where I was going. Somehow, I had to break free from the habit of pleasing everyone except myself.

When I was growing up, my parents merely wanted me to finish school and then graduate from university. But I now know that you don't necessarily earn high pay by having a university degree; these days you need a lot more than just a qualification; you need connections, networks, life experience and charisma. You need to present yourself effectively by dressing well and, as a woman, learning how to apply make-up properly. You need tools to support your physical, mental, financial and spiritual health. All this affects the jobs you land and the sort of life you end up living.

I want you to have exactly what I want for myself: *the most amazing life you can envisage*. I want this book to inspire you to dream bigger, take up space, use your voice, and be your highest

Good Girl

self.

When I was sixteen, I started working freelance jobs. Without any help or connections, I "hustled" my way and managed to get work. From ages sixteen to 20 I worked part-time for a radio station, giving callers relationship advice. People would call in and complain about their partners and ask me my opinion. I'd say, "It doesn't sound as if you guys are compatible." I pretty much just told everybody to break up! What did I know – I was only sixteen!

I also worked as an MC for some time, hosting several shows: big events, launches and concerts, as well as doing voiceover work. It's rare for Cambodians to speak both English and Cambodian fluently and without a strong accent. Although I do have a bit of an accent speaking English, it's not too noticeable. By the time I was seventeen, I was fluent in American English, thanks to MTV and pop culture, and I found myself doing voiceovers for shampoo ads, for example, and recording automatic messages for a telecommunications company's customer care-line. "The number you've dialled is not connected"... ah, what a memory!

I was "hustling" hard. Looking back, I didn't get all this work because I was amazing or driven, but because I was rebelling against authority. I wanted to be my own authority. The authorities in my life had taught me that I should be funded by a *man*, that I should be a housewife, sweet and toned down, keeping my voice low. But because I have a rebellious side, I thought, "Nope, I'm going to go out and do the things I want to do."

When I was eighteen I got a job for six months, working in hospitality at a hotel. I quickly realised it wasn't for me – there were lots authoritative figures and politics, and I had a problem with authority back then. I don't any more, by the way – these days I can spot bad authority immediately and distance myself

You are your environment

from it. And when I recognise good authority, I am happy to sit down, be humble and learn. I'm privileged to now be in a space where I have enough experience and resources not to have to deal often with toxic authority.

Eventually I met my first true love, who turned out to be the most amazing, supportive person to me and our daughter. He and I knew of each other in middle school but we never spoke. He moved to Australia when he was twelve, and we later reconnected on an online platform, Hi5, when I was nineteen. As we had the same extended circle of friends, he and I struck up a friendship, then started hanging out more. He was very encouraging of my entrepreneurial leanings. To any concept I came up with, he would respond, "Good idea, do that." And he'd help me through it, walk me through the process, even fund some of my businesses. But the ideas, the drive, the motivation, the will to do it all – came from me.

The reason I wanted to be a success was to prove my parents and my aunties wrong: *look at me, I don't need a man!* It might not have been the right motivation to start in business, but it worked in my favour at the time. I was motivated to make things happen, and even though I eventually got married and my husband supported me in some of my businesses, I was the one to start all of them. It was me who went out knocking on doors, who designed the business plans, who went to China to buy clothes and was brave enough to see it through when I had no idea where to even begin. For many years I didn't give myself any credit, but I do now.

As I've mentioned, I didn't start my journey with the best mindset, and my advice is not to start a business just because you want to get rich. Yes, money can solve a lot of problems, but it's preferable to start a business because you want to build a

Good Girl

better future for yourself and others. If you're lying awake at 3 a.m., wondering why you're doing what you're doing and you can't come up with an answer, you're likely to fail. You need a strong enough reason to do it or you'll stumble and fall. If your reason for starting a business is just to make loads of money and drive a Lamborghini, you possibly will get there but you won't be "happy" for long.

Suddenly I had more than 100,000 followers.

When I was expecting my daughter eight years ago, I was huge in size. There I was, eight months pregnant – big, bored and working at home from my phone. To alleviate my boredom, I'd make use of my free time each day by dressing up in fabulous outfits, taking pictures of myself and posting them on social media. It turned out people were really inspired by my "pregnant women" fashion – they absolutely loved it! And that's how I went "viral". Before I knew it, I had more than 100,000 followers. This all happened in the space of three short months, and while the response was enormously positive and exciting, it's also what tipped me over the edge in my mental health. Imagine, I was getting all this attention, and then suddenly people were posting comments saying I was a gold-digger and that I had a sugar-daddy. I was 28 and my daughter's father was also 28, but the harsh comments got to me; they deeply affected my self-esteem and led me to believe I was less than I was. The fact that I didn't have a solid support network or good friends also played a part in fuelling the depression that followed.

Fast-forward a couple of years. At 30 years old, I was a millionaire. I had a city apartment with an amazing view, I had businesses, I had a family – and I felt suicidal.

My point is that money is not the end goal; I followed that

You are your environment

path, and it was a mistake. To chase money and fame for the wrong reasons – in order to prove people wrong and seek validation – isn't the path to long-lasting fulfilment. If you want to start a venture, by all means do so, but do it because it aligns with your values.

I understand that entrepreneurship isn't something that will work for everyone. Some people like the security and the regularity of going to work at 9 a.m. and finishing at 5 p.m., having a set salary and a defined number of leave days per year. If that describes you, it doesn't mean this book isn't for you; it just applies to you in a different way.

Something I tend to do in my work is put myself in very sticky situations. I just dive right into the deep end – to me, that's the best way to learn. And then I always trust my instincts to enable me to come out of those situations. I know I'll find a way to emerge somehow! What I do in my working life is risky, and if you have the drive, by all means try it too. But if you don't have that type of personality, don't do it. Just do what feels aligned with where you are going. Do what feels right for you.

I know I'm very different from most other people my age. This is probably because I've had different more experience than most others my age, and because I think differently about life in general. For example, the reason I dive right into sticky situations is because I've befriended the reality that we'll all die one day. I think about death every single day, in a positive way; it's a powerful tool for me. I accept that it will happen and I'm therefore not fearful of it. If tomorrow was my last day I would want to make the most of it. So why fear it?

What to know when you're in a rut

My goal in this book is to help you shift your mindset from a state of negativity to one of empowerment and happiness. I'll draw from my own experiences in a very honest way to show you that you're not alone, and I'll share what I did to shift things, to help you do things differently and climb out of your rut.

I want to help you out of the hole we sometimes all dig ourselves into. It's part of the human experience, so don't feel bad about it. And know that if I could get myself out of a hole and into a good place, so can you.

When you've sunk into a depressive state, you need to find a way out. I know that place – it's one of apathy, low mood and low energy, where everything seems too hard. When you're sad, nothing seems possible. You might think, "I want to go Bali." Then you immediately squash that thought: "No, I can't go to Bali. I don't have the money," or "I want to see my friends" ("I can't do that – I'm not happy") or "I want to be friends with that girl. She seems cool." ("I'm not cool – I can't.")

If you're in that place of "no, no, no", please stick with me. I want to show you what life can be without the negative perspective. Without those endless limitations and restrictions in your head, without the "lies", life will start to open up. Today, I truly love myself and my life, and that hasn't happened because I'm lucky or because I'm the chosen one or anything like that. No, I work

What to know when you're in a rut

really hard for what I have. I throw myself into unconventional situations because that's where I'll grow, I trust my instincts to guide me, and I practise my Five Foundations of Life to keep myself on track.

If you feel overwhelmed, if you feel you're not coping with life, here's a thought: perhaps it's not just about you. If you're a woman, let's look at some gender-related reasons why you might be feeling the way you do.

There's a lot of pressure on women today. For example, we're expected to look beautiful, but not *too* beautiful. We're also expected to keep the house clean and organise meals, but sometimes also provide half the income to support the family. And if we don't have partners, the financial burden is often 100 percent on us to pay the bills and feed and clothe our children. And if you don't have children? You might be struggling to find a partner, feeling stressed because your biological clock is ticking, wondering, "What's wrong with me? Everyone else is married and I'm not!" And in the workplace, even though we're heading towards equal rights and equal opportunities, we're not there yet. Women don't get equal pay; that's a fact. If you state your opinion you might be perceived as too bossy, and if you're too meek, then you're seen as not assertive or serious enough. The reality is that the world we live in isn't made for women to thrive. Back in the day, a woman's job was to support a man and look after the children and the home, but these days we pretty much do everything.

When all these expectations are placed on women, it's no wonder we sometimes feel we're going insane. Of course, men have their own sets of difficulties and expectations, pressures being placed on them by the current confusing society. In fact, men have the highest rate of suicide, some of them resulting

Good Girl

from extremes within the feminist movement and from toxic masculinity. Sometimes there's no space for men to be men, for a man to open a door for a woman, for example. (They can still open doors for me, thank you!)

But society is set up so that a woman has to try twice as hard as a man. Say you're going on a date: you're expected to be well dressed and well groomed, which might entail getting your hair cut and coloured, having a manicure, using make-up and wearing an outfit that accentuates your best features. That's a few 100 dollars here, another couple of 100 there. It all adds up. And men have a few shirts and one suit, and that one suit works for everything, right? (I know I'm exaggerating.) And we don't get equal pay! Only three percent of CEOs globally are female. *Three percent*. This is our reality.

Then there are complicating issues, such as hormones. After three years of therapy, I figured out why I don't like working for other people. One of the reasons is that I have ADHD (attention-deficit/hyperactivity disorder), which was only diagnosed recently. To complicate things, I also have PMDD: premenstrual dysphoric disorder. This is a severe extension of premenstrual syndrome (PMS) and includes a whole range of physical and behavioural symptoms that, thankfully, usually resolve when menstruation starts. Some of the symptoms are extreme sadness, hopelessness, irritability and anger, as well as the commonly known PMS symptoms like breast tenderness and bloating. It's PMS multiplied by a thousand! Every month, I have just two weeks where I'm able to function normally. During the week before my period, I'll have little mental breakdowns. Say I buy some takeaway food and the server forgets to give me the sauce; I'll break down and wail, "God, why is this happening to me?" (Try to imagine my dramatic, sobbing voice.) Then after

What to know when you're in a rut

I've eaten, I'll think, "Hey, why was I so emotional?" There's a notion that if women are angry that means they are "crazy or "emotional". My response is: why do we judge women for verbally expressing their anger when it's perfectly acceptable for men to do so? And sometimes what may seem like an irrational reaction from a woman may just be a result of particular hormones.

We are biologically different from men. If you're a mother and your baby wakes every two hours, you don't get a full night's sleep and you don't produce enough hormones to function well during the day. Women are much more likely to report sleep problems, according to the National Sleep Foundation in the United States.[8] Our hormones are a significant factor: hormonal changes can disrupt sleep when they spike or drop during our menstrual cycle, during and after pregnancy, and around menopause, for instance. And not sleeping well can negatively affect our hormone production. It's a vicious circle.

The first step is to get out of survival mode.

If you are depressed or anxious, if you're feeling "down" or constantly worried much of the time, you are neck-deep in survival mode. You're just doing the basics to stay alive. And the truth is that you simply cannot create from a place of survival.

On a physiological level, when we're in survival mode the sympathetic nervous system is activated. In human evolution this is a survival mechanism to help us in life-threatening situations: our muscles tense up so they're ready for action, our breathing quickens, and our heart pounds to supply our body with more

---

8   Refer to www.sleepfoundation.org for academic papers outlining this gendered difference.

energy – we are revved up and on high alert. This is our body's "fight or flight" system, and it contrasts with the parasympathetic nervous system, which is the body's "rest and digest" or "feed and breed" system.

Normally, once a threat or stressor has passed – whether it's a near-collision on the freeway or a job interview, our levels of the stress hormone cortisol fall and our parasympathetic nervous system acts like a car brake, dampening the stress response.

So, usually there's an interplay between the two systems and they balance each other out, but when we're consistently stressed, anxious or depressed, the sympathetic nervous system can be *continually* activated, *without* the normal counteracting effect of the parasympathetic nervous system. What does this do to us? It can lead to migraines, back pain, arthritis, the drive to overeat or binge, digestive problems, muscular pain, heart issues, using drugs or drink to "self-medicate", and a whole lot more. Basically, it wears us out because it's not how our minds or bodies were designed to operate.

We cannot craft a good life for ourselves until we exit survival mode. So the first step is to get out of it. How do we do that?

My Five Foundations of Life

This is my blueprint for a good life. I believe everyone needs these five elements:

- The first Foundation is **Physical**: we need to get our body moving, feel physically healthy and be free of pain.
- The second Foundation is **Mental & Emotional**: we need to nourish our mind, learning something new every day and managing our feelings.
- The third Foundation is **Community**: we need people

who support us, whether family, friends or both. This is about relationships and it includes our relationship with ourselves: honouring ourselves and not being people-pleasers.
- The fourth Foundation is **Spiritual**: we need a sense of something bigger than ourselves, something we can have faith in – God, the universe or whatever makes sense to us individually.
- The fifth Foundation is **Financial**: we need money and resources, even if we think they're not important.

If you want to know how to get out of survival mode, I suggest you work on each of the Five Foundations daily. This will give you a structure for living. In fact, if you do ten minutes from each of the Five Foundations every day for two weeks, you may well find your life becoming more purposeful.

Finally, I want you to know that there is light at the end of the tunnel. You need to keep taking one step forward, then another step and another, secure in the knowledge that a beautiful, fulfilling life can be yours. No matter what you've been through and how hard you've been hit, your trauma doesn't have to have the final word. You are not alone, even if you think you are. Things are in perpetual motion, and that means there is always hope.

Ready? Let's get started.

Foundation 1: Physical

The physical is often the first thing we let slide. But it's also the easiest one to restart.

Flashback to 2017. I'm in bed and I can't get up. My daughter is four months old and I'm feeling very depressed. Since giving birth I feel like I haven't really moved at all, and I'm used to not going out of the house or engaging with the outside world. My world has moved indoors. I put on a lot of weight during my pregnancy, 22 kilograms, and now I don't want to get out of bed at all. I have a cough, so I drink cough syrup, and after that I doze off. It's not like falling asleep; I just get knocked out by the cough syrup and doze. It's a nice feeling, the ability to just drift away. I wake up and feed my daughter, take care of her, and then I drink more cough syrup and doze again, and later I go back to sleep fully. I don't want to move my body. In only a week, my life has been reduced to this; it's been a domino effect. My depressive state has grown and grown – and now I'm stuck. I'm not able to get up any more. I just can't.

Fast-forward a few years. I'm at my physical peak and it feels amazing. I've just been at the gym for a two-hour workout, one hour of weight training and an hour of boxing, and I'm walking

Foundation 1: Physical

around feeling like anything is possible. Whatever this day can throw at me, I can take it! I train three to four times a week. Boxing is more than a physical experience for me; it gives me a mental lift. Afterwards I have all the confidence in the world – secretly I'd love to punch the f*&k out of someone; "come at me, bro!" I love lifting heavy weights too. As I'm keen on spearfishing, I do exercises to build my upper-body strength: lifting dumbbells, pulling weights on strings. You need this strength when you're loading a metre-long speargun underwater because you've got to pull the gun towards your chest through all that water resistance. It's physically taxing, especially when you're in deep and looking for the big fish. And it feels so empowering to have the strength to load my speargun myself and not have to hand it to someone else to load for me. I'm feeling on top of the world, and I'll carry this energy throughout the day.

"Wow, that must be nice for you Piyané, but I don't have two hours to work out – plus I can't afford it!" I know, I know. Stay with me here...

Start with gratitude for your body.

Have you ever looked at your hands and thought, "Wow, look at these tools I was born with?" I'm studying my hands right now: these fingerprints are unique; there's no one else like me in the world. And these thumbs can do amazing things for me, including scrolling all day on my phone if I choose to.

Our body is the thing we most take for granted. Many of us act as if we're going to live forever, but of course we're not. Death will come, though probably (hopefully) not today. Until it does, your body is all you have. This physical body is a miraculous vessel that was created to carry out experiences for you. Everything you decide to do, your body materialises. It carries you everywhere

Good Girl

you want to go. If you tell your body to take you from point A to point B, without you even thinking whether your left or right foot should step first, your body's already walking you there. It's amazing: you don't have to press any buttons to make this happen.

Most people never stop to think that their heart beats for them, day in and day out. And it does this without us even telling it to. Also, even when I was suicidal and wanted my heart to stop beating, it didn't. It just kept on beating steadily, doing its job. We also breathe in and out, day and night, without having to instruct our body to do so. Regardless of what we think or say, our body is programmed by DNA to perform a whole symphony of helpful actions for us. When I was pregnant and my daughter was growing inside my belly, every time I ate something, I'd think something like, "Hey, I just made an eyeball today! No wonder I'm feeling tired." That truly felt miraculous: I never told my body to make my daughter's eyeballs, to make her ears, to grow her heart. I didn't have to, because each gene has its job description and dutifully carries it out.

When I cut or injure myself, I don't have to tell my body to heal; it heals by itself. When I sleep, I don't have to monitor my breathing; I'm so blessed that my body does it for me. Taking all this into account, it seems that the least I can do is give my body the resources it needs to function properly. My body is already working hard enough to keep me alive and well; I don't need to make its job any harder. In fact, giving it the right working conditions is the only thing I *can* control. Everything else is automated and beyond my control.

Let's start with appreciation and gratitude for our bodies. Let's say "thank you" to our body; if you are religious, consider saying a prayer for it. *Thank you so much for creating me, for giving me this*

Foundation 1: Physical

vessel in which to experience life. My soul experiences life through this body because of you. Whatever force out there created me, thank you. I do not have to think about my heart beating, I do not have to think about breathing; my body does it for me. I am so grateful for everything it does.

The truth is that we often take advantage of our physical selves. We abuse our bodies, and it often begins in unremarkable little ways. Usually it doesn't start with us going for eight days straight without sleep, for instance, or taking fifteen plane flights without neck support, or missing three consecutive meals because we're just too busy, or by doing heavy drugs. Mistreating our body starts in very small ways – perhaps not drinking enough water because we feel too busy to go to the bathroom. Or, instead of having lunch at 12, postponing it to 1.30 p.m. Or going to bed at midnight instead of at 10. It may start innocuously like this, but eventually you can end up where I am at the moment. As I'm recording notes for this book, I'm lying down on a bed while therapists are performing a treatment on my body because I have a painful kink in my neck. I've been stressed for a few weeks and my body is showing the signs.

The truth is that I'm often unable to slow down because of my ADHD. The beauty of ADHD is that I can be hyper-focussed, which is both a blessing and a curse; when I'm hyper-focussed, I can do many things at once, which is what enables me to run multiple businesses and work on different projects concurrently. But let's talk about being focussed and losing track of time. Even if you don't have ADHD I'm sure you can relate to this, because when we're engrossed in an activity we enjoy, we all tend to forget time. If you're a gamer, you'll know how quickly time passes when you're playing your favourite games. If you love movies, how you forget time completely when you're engrossed in a new movie.

Good Girl

The problem with being hyper-focussed is that you tend to forget your physical state. If you're like me, you can easily sit in one position looking at your phone, scrolling addictively through social media, and before you know it two or three hours have passed. Now you've been stuck in one position for hours, your neck bent and your arm raised – ouch! – and you're suddenly aware that you're sitting in a cold room because it's late at night and you forgot to turn on the heater; if you're in Asia, you have probably forgotten to turn on the air-conditioning so now you're sweating in a stifling hot room. By the time you tune back into your physical body, it's out of balance and in pain.

Unfortunately, the body is the first thing we take advantage of because it doesn't have a say. It just does what we tell it to do. The problems start when we don't consistently take care of this primary vessel, by eating badly or not getting enough sleep, for instance. It starts to retaliate. Our body slows down and we feel the effects of our lifestyle. This state can be difficult to reverse, but please know that it's never too late. At the very least, we can slow down the effects of an unhealthy lifestyle; we can also pause the damage we have caused to our body, and even reverse it with the right treatments.

The first Foundation in the book is Physical because this is often the easiest one to let slide. Thankfully, it's also the one that's easiest to get a handle on. Once I couldn't get out of bed; now I'm flying around the world, running multiple businesses. You might think, "Hang on, this can't be the same person. How on earth did she get from there to here?" These are the guidelines that got me up and running (or at least walking) again.

Foundation 1: Physical

TIPS AND TOOLS

Before we dive in, I have a little task for you. If you are a banker or an accountant, or have run a business before, you might be familiar with the concept of Assessment and Audit. Sounds fancy and complicated, right? It's not. Before we dive into the nitty gritty of the tips that can get you back on your feet, I want you to assess and audit your life. You can download an Assessment and Audit form from **www.piyane.com/resources**. This is a sheet of paper to fill in where you are completely honest with me (but most importantly, with yourself). After all, without fail, the only resource humans have equally, is Time. I want you to fill in what you have done over the last 24 hours, being totally and completely honest. Yes, even the time you spent scrolling on your phone and how much water you drank. There's no shame here. I only ask that you do this because, just like a banker, you can't make sound investments if you are unclear about the resources, the amounts spent and what you spent it on. Then changes can be made accordingly. Be very detailed; write everything down. You may pause your reading or listening to this book to do this exercise and come back later. Or you might choose to keep going to the end, but please come back to do this because it is necessary. We can't change what we don't know. Don't be ashamed of what you write down. Own it and embrace it, knowing you are taking the first step to taking your life back by the balls.

Here are a few basic but absolutely necessary things that must be in your day audit. If you leave them out, it's okay too.

Your time audit looks something like this. Vary the times according to when you get up and go to bed.

Good Girl

Piyané Ung

Time Audit:

6am

7am

8am

9am

10am

11am

12pm

1pm

2pm

3pm

4pm

5pm

6pm

7pm

8pm

9pm

Foundation 1: Physical

In the next chapters I will introduce my personal daily journal that helps me commit to and track all of the new structures in my life. It's quick and easy, you just need commitment and faith in it. If you don't have these things, you're welcome to borrow my faith. You've got this! My coach gifted me this faith, when I was lost and totally broken. She said, "Piyané, borrow my faith." So here I am, paying her gift forward – if you don't have faith of your own, please take mine.

Drink two to three litres of water daily.

Let's start with the most basic factor: hydration. Water is fundamental to our health because our bodies are 60 percent water. When we drink enough water during the day, we can avoid headaches, migraines, feeling irritated and edgy and a slew of other problems. Water helps to regulate manifold processes in the body and flushes out toxins, including cortisol after a stressful episode.

How much water did you drink today? (I know, I sound like your mother when you were little, but she did have a point!) Two litres per day is my minimum. Find one of those big, beautiful water bottles to fill and keep it on your desk or in your kitchen – a place where you'll see it. Yes, you'll pee more often but it's worth it. Please don't avoid drinking water just so you won't have to go to the bathroom! My trick is to drink a lot of water when I wake up; I'll easily drink a litre and a half within the first fifteen minutes of waking. People say you shouldn't drink water just before bed, but I do. Consult with experts and consult with your body: if drinking water at night reduces the quality of your sleep because you have to wake up and go to the bathroom, it's probably not a good idea for you. Just do what works.

Sometimes your body can't tell the difference between being

hungry and thirsty: often you'll want to eat when what you really need is a big dose of water. I'm not someone who usually craves sugar, but when I do occasionally get a yearning for Coca-Cola, I ask myself, "Do I really want Coke or is it water that I need?" Then I'll take a sip of water and realise I actually needed a big drink of water to rehydrate myself.

Because I'm telling you this, does it mean that I drink two to three litres of water every day? Unfortunately not – but when I remember the importance of it, I do drink plenty of water. The importance of keeping your body hydrated cannot be overstated. If your body doesn't function properly, neither does anything else; your mental health doesn't function properly, your financial health doesn't either, and perhaps not even your spiritual health. And, if your body isn't performing optimally, your connection to your community won't be strong, because you'll be unable to contribute effectively. So this first Foundation is fundamental to the functioning of all the other Foundations. Getting this one right is about making small shifts. For instance, can you drink water between your coffees during the day? Little changes like these add up and make a big difference.

Here are my hydration guidelines:

- **Drink two to three litres of water every day**.
- **Drink filtered water**. There's so much research about why water should be filtered. Water filtration removes impurities, bacteria and chemicals added during the treatment process. Impurities include particles such as soil, rust, sand and sediment; and chemicals like chlorine and fluoride are added to public water supplies to kill bacteria and viruses. Traces of pharmaceuticals have been found in tap water, as well as industrial chemicals

Foundation 1: Physical

occasionally, such as herbicides, pesticides and organic chemicals. Filtration also removes traces of heavy metals, which can cause health problems. Exposure to unhealthy levels of lead has been linked to nervous system damage and other health issues; copper is particularly dangerous for young children and excessive exposure in adults can cause gastrointestinal distress, liver issues and kidney damage. Long-term exposure to high concentrations of mercury can affect children and cause kidney damage in adults.

- **Don't drink water out of a plastic bottle** if you can help it. It's not the end of the world if you do – I drank water from one today – but if you have the choice, don't. Bottled water can contain microplastics, and each bottle contributes to the plastic pollution problem.

Right now, I feel very dehydrated. I know I should drink some water but I'm lying on a bed having treatment for my neck, which I've abused over the last couple of weeks because I've been on planes virtually non-stop. I took four flights last week, this week I've taken two flights, and next week I'll be taking four flights again. They're not very long flights, but flying in a plane is not comfortable for anybody. You're stuck sitting in an upright position, the air is extremely dehydrating, and afterwards the body takes time to recover. Note to self: drink water!

Get enough sleep.

Another confession: I sometimes abuse my body by not going to sleep on time. (I'm sharing information like this to give you a glimpse into the reality of my life, and because you might relate to it. I wonder how you abuse your own body?) I don't go to sleep

Good Girl

on time every day because I have many events to attend. My primary way of expanding my businesses is to involve investors, and for that to happen, I need to keep up appearances. I also enjoy having conversations with people – everyone has a story and I love hearing them, so I'm not complaining here. It's ideal to go to bed at roughly the same time each night, and I don't always do that because of my lifestyle – I don't have the same schedule every day. For example, two nights ago I was at a gala dinner. I left at 11 p.m., and by the time I'd got home and taken off the many layers of my outfit and the million bobby pins from my hair, and showered and removed my make-up, it was 12.30 – or was it 1 a.m.? So that's when I went to bed, and the next morning I had a meeting at 8 o'clock. I had six and a half hours' sleep that night, which isn't nearly enough for me.

Everybody has different sleep needs: while some people need seven to eight hours of sleep, I need eight hours at the very least. Needless to say I have some work to do in this area; my lifestyle will have to change to accommodate my sleep schedule. This is my struggle – so please don't feel bad if you also can't commit to this just yet. If you can't do so now, please set the intention to commit when you can. Get eight hours of sleep as often as possible. If you have insomnia, consider speaking to a doctor to find a way around it. This is a priority. Sleep is when your brain gets to compartmentalise and store long-term memories. Don't underestimate the impact of a lack of sleep. There's a reason why sleep deprivation is used as a form of torture – it's really effective in breaking a person down.

Get into the habit of avoiding screens before bed. Your brain is a computer and needs time to shut down properly and file away information from the events of the day. Blue light in the form of TV, computer and phone screens is disruptive to sleep, so avoid it for

Foundation 1: Physical

two to three hours before bedtime if you can, as the professionals advise, or at least an hour before bed.

Even if you're feeling the first signs of sleepiness at night, if you keep scrolling through online news your body will soon be jacked with cortisol. There's a lot of bad news out there: you might not necessarily be feeling stressed in your own life, but seeing a report about a war that has flared up again, for instance, or that a celebrity you follow is having a huge fight with someone, can affect your mental and physical state. Suddenly you're feeling angry, shocked, outraged – and being flooded with the stress hormone cortisol at 11 p.m. is going to disrupt your sleep. Instead, find a routine that will protect you from distressing news and allow your body and mind to ease into bedtime. Decide the time when you will switch off your phone each night; then time becomes *your* time.

Nap if you can.

I can't overstress the importance of listening to your body. As much as possible, rest when you are tired. Recently I've picked up the habit of having an afternoon nap. You may not be able to take fifteen minutes of shut-eye in the early afternoon, as I just have. You know I quit the nine-to-five world at age eighteen to pursue my dream of being an entrepreneur, but now it feels like I'm often on the go for 20 hours a day! My power naps last anything from fifteen minutes to half an hour. I refuse to feel guilty about them: research shows that napping can extend your lifespan.

People often tell me they can't nap during the day because they'll end up sleeping for two to three hours. I used to be the same. My advice is to try setting an alarm so you don't oversleep; you can also train your mind to wake you after a certain time, telling yourself, "Wake me at 4.20 so I sleep for 20 minutes." It actually works.

Even if you don't sleep, have a rest. Lie down completely still for fifteen minutes and you'll emerge feeling refreshed. This downtime provides a healthy balance to all the activity we do in a day.

Give yourself grace.

I have introduced water and sleep as fundamental factors to your well-being, and have also told you these are both things I don't do consistently. Yet advising you to do them doesn't mean that I'm a hypocrite. It just means I'm human, and I give myself the grace to understand that I can't always follow sound lifestyle advice to the letter. When I can I do so, around 80 to 90 percent of the time, my life looks like what I outline in this book: disciplined, healthy and on track.

But then there's the 10 to 20 percent, which is where I am right now. My approach during these erratic times – when I get to bed late and don't drink enough water and stray in other ways from the Foundations – is to be gracious with myself.

Having grown up in a household without much privacy, I often feel as if I don't have my own space. Sometimes I ask myself, "Am I an extrovert or an introvert?" Those who know me will tell you I'm very talkative: I'm chatty and often strike up conversations with strangers, because I absolutely love hearing people's stories. But in truth, I feel more of an introvert. Part of me likes to stay up late at night, and it's been that way for years, long before I started my self-development journey. I would go to bed very late at night because that felt like the only time I could truly be alone and recharge. In the peace and silence when others were asleep, I could take a deep breath, decompress, mentally declutter and just be me. So that tendency lingers and sometimes gets in the

Foundation 1: Physical

way of my intention to go to bed at 10 p.m. each night.

Find a healthy eating plan.

I am neither a nutritionist nor an expert in physical health, so the information I'm sharing with you comes mostly from personal experience. If you can afford to, consult a professional when it comes to finding the right eating plan for you. If not, fortunately we live in an era where so much is available at the touch of a button: search Google and YouTube to find a healthy eating plan that suits you; one that is sustainable and delicious. It may take time to get your eating on track, but it's worth investing the time to get it right for you.

No one knows your body better than you do. Observe your body and what it's telling you it needs. Unlike many people, I only eat two meals a day. I've practised intermittent fasting for 20 years; having dinner and not eating until the following afternoon. If I eat breakfast I feel mentally foggy in the morning, and over time my body has adapted to this. This is what's normal for me and my body. I don't practise intermittent fasting because I'm highly disciplined but rather because it's what works for me.

Move for ten minutes daily.

If you're feeling low, the last thing you feel like doing is moving your body. I get it. It's a Catch-22: you need to go out to not feel depressed, but when you're depressed you don't feel like going out. But let me tell you something: you *need* to go out. When we are depressed we need to move; we need to go outside, because that gets the endorphins flowing through our system. Endorphins are the natural hormones that make us feel good. When they're moving through our body – and just ten minutes gets them going

– our mind shifts a little.

Listen to your excuses rising: *I'm so overweight I can't run!* It doesn't matter. You can walk. *I don't have the money to go to the gym!* Just open YouTube. There's a whole world of exercises you can do at home, barefoot, even without the need for a mat.

Start small – with just ten minutes or five minutes or even two minutes of physical movement, and it's highly likely you'll feel better. When I finally got myself out of bed and followed the advice to exercise, I went to the gym and half an hour later I thought, "Oh... what happened there? For a short while, I forgot to be depressed." I told myself I could always go back to being depressed if the exercise trick didn't work. But it did. So I kept doing it, just a bit every day. And it kept working. Exercise releases a range of feel-good chemicals: dopamine and endorphins, which reduce stress and boost your sense of well-being.

Being physical doesn't have to mean plunging into an extreme fitness regime or forcing yourself to do a form of exercise you don't enjoy. For example, you can move your body slowly, such as Tai Chi, simply appreciating that you have a physical body; being aware that you are here, now, in this space, in this moment. That can be a beautiful physical experience. Or you can do stretches in bed, as I sometimes do. Start with what's manageable for you. Don't begin with a bells-and-whistles membership with the top trainer at the most expensive gym. Don't spend fifteen hours looking for gym outfits. As human beings, we like to distract ourselves with pastimes like shoe-shopping. Don't use your credit card on any of this!

Take a cold shower or bath.

This is one of my great vitality tricks. I try to do it every day, but that's a lot easier in Melbourne, where ice-cold water comes

Foundation 1: Physical

out of the cold tap; in hot Cambodia, the "cold" water is warm, which means I have to buy ice for a cold bath. I aim to do this a few times a week, especially after a workout, as it releases soreness from the muscles after exercise. "Cold therapy", even just switching from a warm to a cold shower for a couple of minutes, has a number of physical and mental benefits. It can improve your circulation, boost your immunity against common viruses like colds, combat symptoms of depression by reducing anxiety and boosting your mood, raise your metabolism, reduce inflammation and muscular soreness, and relieve localised pain.

No more excuses. You do have ten minutes a day to spend on yourself.

If your self-confidence is low, you need to get out and do something about it. Sign up to the gym, for example. And if you lack the time or money for that, there's plenty you can do in just ten to fifteen minutes at home. If your immediate response to that is, "I'm a very busy mother! I don't have time!" that certainly is a problem. If you don't have ten minutes for yourself each day, that speaks volumes about why you picked up this book. It suggests you may be a people-pleaser. You're probably "pleasing" your family, your children, your boss: everyone except yourself.

I dare you to do this: pick up your cell-phone and locate the records of your internet usage, where your time on various apps is tracked each day. You'll probably see Instagram, Facebook, TikTok, YouTube, and you'll see that your time spent here daily is a bit (or a lot) more than ten minutes.

No more excuses. You *do* have ten minutes a day.

But perhaps you don't want to start because it's scary – and I can understand that. Thinking about your physical goals can seem overwhelming. *What do I want to achieve? Do I want to*

Good Girl

be fitter? Do I want to lose 10 kilograms? Or 20 kilograms? When you ponder these weighty questions, the journey suddenly seems long and gloomy and you're filled with dread because now you have to take the first step.

I get it. I have many friends who weren't happy with their weight. Some of them lost a lot of weight – and regained it. This is a struggle many people face: some people have a disordered relationship with food, or an addiction to food, which is a really tough one. With other addictions, like smoking or vaping, drugs, alcohol or gambling, you can avoid them, even though it's hard. You can throw away your cigarettes or vape, you can get rid of your drugs and bottles of alcohol, you can stop visiting casinos and block those sites on your phone – they just need to stay out of sight. But you cannot avoid food. We have to eat every day to stay alive. So if food is your issue, I have full compassion for you. It's best to seek help from Overeaters Anonymous or a professional who can offer you the support you need.

Embarrassment is the entry fee for achievement.

You'll get there as long as you're willing to pay the price: embarrassment. I know that you might not want to join the gym, hire a personal trainer or attend a support group meeting because it feels too embarrassing. Let me tell you something important: embarrassment is the price of entry if you want to achieve anything. In fact, it's the fee for pretty much everything you might wish to attain or master in this world. For example, if you dream of being an entrepreneur, you'll have to walk into a room to network with strangers and ask questions and run the risk of looking like an idiot. If you want to be an author, you'll have to find out how to write the book you feel is inside you and eventually show people what you've written. Embarrassment is

Foundation 1: Physical

the fee. You will always be embarrassed at your first show. You will always be embarrassed the first time you perform. You will always be embarrassed the first time you start a business. Get used to it, because you have to pay the fees wherever you go. We all do. And if people judge you, they're not your people anyway.

At **www.piyane.com/resources**, you can download a guide to keeping a daily journal to set and track your goals for all five Foundations, including physical.

Doing something for the Physical Foundation daily isn't just about exercising your body; this is a mental exercise to help you grow in respect for yourself. When you committed to doing physical exercise for two minutes yesterday, and you did it again today, by tomorrow you'll be feeling excited that you've kept the practice up for three days. Now you're making progress in developing a good habit. You'll think, "Oo, maybe I can do three minutes. Or ten. Maybe I can even start going to the gym." What we're doing is building mental confidence in ourselves.

Here's a confession: I'll go for weeks at a time without working on my Five Foundations. This is what has happened lately, and it's why I'm back in a rut. And it's okay. Pick yourself up and start doing it again. Once your daily "Foundations" work has become an integral part of your life, don't assume you can just list your daily goals in your head each day. I find I need to write them down, on paper or in a book. When my intentions are in a tangible form, they feel different from when they're merely notes on my phone. Written goals seem more real and I'm more likely to act on them.

Start feeling better, by yourself, from the inside.

Since we're all in different states of physical wellness, any discussion about our bodies will no doubt touch a nerve with some of us. Let me be clear: I'm completely in favour of body

Good Girl

positivity. I understand that for some people, hormonal issues and genetic conditions might mean the body is unable to digest food properly, for instance. What I'm saying is *do what you can*. I'm not interested in judging the size of your waist, your breasts or hips or the number on your scales; what I'm interested in is that mental space when you look at yourself in the mirror and don't feel happy. Whether other people think you're good-looking or smart doesn't matter to me; what I care about is your answer to questions like these:

- Is this the best you've felt in this body?
- If you keep going the way you are, are you more likely to be healthier and happier in your skin?

These are deeply difficult questions for many of us. If you're psychologically healthy with no people-pleasing tendencies, you might not find these questions uncomfortable. You might not think this book can teach you anything – and that's fantastic. Some people are born with a high degree of grit and resilience and are fortunate enough to be brought up in a family environment that encourages this and empowers them. When your parents, grandparents, aunts, uncles and cousins regularly tell you that you're beautiful and smart, you grow up believing it.

But we're not all in that boat. In Cambodia it's called the "crab effect": as soon as one little crab starts crawling up out of the basket, another crab tries to pull it down and climb up instead. In Australia it's called "Tall Poppy Syndrome". The truth is that many of us are born into an environment where others try to dim our light if they think we shine too brightly or take up too much space. When you've experienced that, unfortunately you can grow up with thoughts like, "I'm not good enough", "I'm not good-looking enough", "I'm not smart enough". For some, these thoughts dominate and escalate to psychological disorders. If you are

Foundation 1: Physical

anorexic, bulimic, have body dysmorphia or any other serious body issue, I urge you to consult a professional for support. This book is not intended as a cure for anyone with serious physical or mental health conditions.

But if you are someone who struggles with low self-esteem – if you look in the mirror and think you deserve better in life – this book *is* for you.

I used to be able to effortlessly run, climb and move like the wind. At present, I can't do any of these things without spraining or hurting something.

There's no amount of coaching or therapy that can make you feel better about yourself unless you start feeling better, by yourself, from the inside. Here's an example from my own life. In Cambodia it's trendy to be white, but I like the golden colour of my skin. What people say doesn't affect me today because I love my skin; it's how I identify myself. Self-esteem starts in your head.

I have already said I put on over 20 kilograms when I was pregnant. I know that may not seem like a lot to other people, but I was used to being a size Small and now I was a Large, and my self-confidence was low as a result. It didn't matter whether friends were saying, "Just focus on body positivity, Piyané!"; I just didn't feel good. I didn't need all that food and excess weight to hold me back. And when I looked in the mirror, I didn't feel happy about myself. So, it doesn't matter what other people are telling you, or whether the trend is towards body positivity and those in your circle are encouraging you to stay big. What matters is when *you don't feel good*. If you look in the mirror and you feel great, you don't have to change a thing. But if you look in the mirror and you don't feel good, do something about it. Either that (and if you decide to get surgery, that's your business) or make peace with the way you are. Have confidence. Look at Barbra Streisand, who was repeatedly told she was talented but too ugly to crack it – she went on to become a world-renowned singer and actress. Make a change for the sake of your mental and physical health, so that when you look in the mirror, you can think, "Hm, I look good! I like what I see."

Hitting rock bottom is good news: there's nowhere else to go but up.

When someone tells me their life is in a bad state, I share what I've learned after hitting rock bottom many times: if you hit rock bottom, that's good news, because it means you have nowhere else to go but up. When you're completely burnt out, drained and done with life, that means you have nothing else to lose.

Eight years ago, when I was 28 and suffering severe post-partum depression, I felt suicidal and didn't want to go out anywhere. By the way, if you think lying in bed all day sounds lovely, believe me, it's not. Lying in bed, depressed, is like a prison. It's not as if I was happily relaxing, watching Netflix; instead I was thinking the world would be better off without me. While looking at the baby girl I'd just brought into the world, instead of feeling happiness and pride, I felt shame – deep, dark shame. "I shouldn't be here because I'm just an embarrassment to her. I'm not a good mother. She'd be better off without me. I'm sure my husband will be able to find a better wife who will look after our daughter better. Because who would want a mother like this? Who'd want to grow up with someone like this? I'll screw her up. I'd rather die."

These are the kind of thoughts I had back then. It took so much willpower for me to get out of bed and regain my previous functioning. I knew I had to sort out my mental state, so I started seeing a therapist, and it felt like an achievement when I could

Foundation 1: Physical

get through the day, doing normal things like brushing my teeth and going out of the house.

At the time, I didn't have guidelines like these to help me through. I hadn't found any books like this to advise me to restore my physical health by doing just ten minutes of exercise a day. Because I was uninformed, I allowed myself to gain 22 kilograms. I wasn't huge by any means, but I was heavy. I'd been 20 kilos lighter just two years before, and I could feel the weight sitting on me. This dramatic weight gain put stress on my back, leading to lower back pain and, because I wasn't happy, I'd often sit in a slumped position, which also gave me neck pain. When I looked in the mirror, I knew I'd hit rock bottom. I had nowhere to go, and that's when I decided I needed to do something about my physical state. I said to myself, "Enough is enough. I'm just going to try this thing that people do – go to the gym." Sure, I had gone to the gym in the past, but I'd never had a personal trainer. So, after two to three years of doing virtually no exercise, I started looking for a body-builder trainer. (As I've said, I like to dive into things.) And I found someone suitable: a woman who was a champion body-builder with an awesome, strong body. I plunged in and overwhelmed myself in the beginning, but over time I adapted. I trained with her for about eight years, only finishing up with her last year.

These days, I feel good in my body even when I'm not going to the gym and lifting weights. But the fact that I stopped training with my body-builder is one reason I'm not in peak physical condition at the moment. Since my intention is to be authentic with you, I'll freely admit that at this point in my life, I am not doing many of the things I'm advising you to do. As I've mentioned, sometimes it's okay to go off track for a few weeks, or even a few months. And I'm in one of those phases currently. Accept it with grace and get started again.

Writing this book is reminding me of all the steps I took a few years ago to get my life rebooted. If anything, I am restarting this journey. Right now, I have my gym clothes with me for the first time in six months. I'm a busy mother, I travel a lot, I don't have much free time – but I'm getting started, because I'm writing this book as much for myself as for you.

Start small and keep going.

I could sit here and feel like a fraud. "Imposter Syndrome" could strike: who am I, Piyané, to write a book about living life well? Actually, I'm a human being, which means life sometimes gets overwhelmingly busy and I go off track for a few months – but I have the ability to get back on track again. The fact that I haven't been going to the gym regularly doesn't mean I'm not moving. In fact, I walk about 10,000 steps a day, not because I'm some super-ambitious person when it comes to setting activity goals, but because where I live it's often easier to walk from A to B, than taking a taxi.

Do you make excuses for yourself? I do, frequently. "It's cold"; "I don't have the right gym clothes": these are excuses that will haunt you later. I'm doing exactly that right now. I'm contemplating going to gym this afternoon, but I'm also feeling tired. Today I had four meetings, then an hour-long call with the tax authority. It's been a long day. My gym clothes are packed, but I could just stay home and take a nap before my dinner tonight...

If you're a new mother, you might lift your baby for a few minutes and consider that a little workout and make excuses for why you don't get to the gym. That's fine for a day; it's fine for two days. But when three days turns into a week in which you've had no physical exercise, it's become a habit. Not going to the

Foundation 1: Physical

gym has become a convenience for you. Stopping prioritising my physical fitness was exactly how I got off track when I was a new mother.

Don't feel bad if you too are making excuses not to exercise. I'm not sitting here judging you. Just be aware of the excuses you make to yourself; be honest. Later on, you'll reach a point where you've had enough of your own excuses and you'll start doing something about it.

When it comes to my diet, I'm quite consistent. I also drink plenty of water and generally get enough sleep. Strength and fitness, however, is where I need to place my effort. It's about asking yourself, "What is my goal? What's the area I need to improve?" Whether your goals are small or big, keep taking little steps each day towards them, in each of the Five Foundations.

An example of a big goal might be "to lose 20 kg". Let's be realistic: you're not going to lose those 20 kg in a month but you can lose them over three years. I can hear you wailing, "Three years! That's so long!" Yes, but if you don't take little steps, in three years' time you won't have lost any weight at all. To achieve that, shift your lifestyle in small ways at a time. Can you switch from Coke to water, for example? Can you walk to appointments instead of driving or taking a taxi or bus? Can you eat a piece of fruit instead of a processed snack every second day? Can you do five minutes of stretching each morning?

All these steps are investments in your body. Wake up and do one or two of them, and you will set the tone for the rest of your day. *You* will positively alter how your day will turn out.

I understand that not all of this is possible all the time. You aren't necessarily going to do a gym workout every day, followed by a bracing cold shower. You're busy and so am I. The key is to start small and keep going, and know when you're in that

Good Girl

peak mode, you'll have a wonderful sense of confidence. When I'm feeling physically strong, I feel empowered on every level; I feel I can handle anything that's thrown at me. Physical exercise isn't just physical; it releases chemicals into our brains and we actually become happier. Research shows that a brisk 30-minute walk or jog three times a week can be just as effective in relieving the symptoms of major depression as antidepressants.[9] Or a 20-minute brisk walk a day five days a week also has the same result.[10] Get moving, raise your heart rate, work up a bit of a sweat and see how different you feel. "Emotion is energy in motion," wrote Neale Donald Walsch.[11] When you're depressed you don't want to run, but when you run you shake off your depression. It's worth a try.

As a reformed people-pleaser, I understand what goes through the mind of someone who has depression or anxiety and a low sense of self-worth. I want to tell you that you're worthy of going to the gym. You're worthy of getting fit and strong. Busy lifestyle aside, if you believe you're worthy enough, you will do it.

If you believe it's always more important to cook a beautiful three-course meal for your family each day, then you'll sacrifice going to the gym for them. This is okay some of the time, but try to balance your family duties with personal priorities so your

---

9   Duke University. "Exercise May Be Just As Effective As Medication For Treating Major Depression." ScienceDaily. ScienceDaily, 27 October 1999., www.sciencedaily.com/releases/1999/10/991027071931.htm.

10 www.medicalnewstoday.com (17 July 2023), citing a ten-year study by Dr Eamon Laird, postdoctoral research fellow at the University of Limerick for Health Research Board (HRB) Ireland.

11 Neale Donald Walsch, *Conversations with God, An Uncommon Dialogue: Living in the World with Honesty, Courage, and Love - Volume 1* (Hachette Australia: 1999).

Foundation 1: Physical

health and sense of self-worth aren't swept aside. I don't go to the gym every day; I aim for three or four days a week. Some people go to the gym every day because that's what works for them. For me, sometimes under "Physical" in my journal, I'll just write "walking". Sometimes it's just "stretching". And on other days, it's simply "stretching in bed": on those occasions I'll do arm, neck and head stretches.

Prioritising yourself can feel strange and difficult at first. "I know I said I was going to work ten minutes a day on my physical health, but this week I've got to focus on this deadline from a client..." Does that sound familiar? I know the feeling. Say I've scheduled a meeting with you for 3 p.m., but when the time draws near, I realise I'm coming down with the 'flu, feeling feverish and rundown, and I'd rather not have the meeting, but I think, "I don't want you to judge me, so I'm just going to show up for the meeting, even though I'm not feeling well." So I'm showing up for you, but I'm not showing up for myself.

This is why it's easy for people not to go to the gym and not to work on their mental health and see a therapist when they need to, and not to have faith and pray. It's easier not to work on planning their financial life. It's easier to watch TV than work on our taxes! If no one's holding us accountable and we don't have self-respect, we won't do the important things that keep our life on track and we can start slipping into a state of depression. It's about keeping our word to ourselves; no one else has to know.

You won't see results straight away after making a change, by the way. But when it comes to exercise, it's the mental strengthening that counts because this forms the blueprint for everything else in your life. If you're working out only to look good to impress other people, the weight will pile back on again. (Sorry to break it to you!) You have to want to do the work for yourself.

Good Girl

You have to want to work because you're sick and tired of where you are now. Put simply, you have to *want* to change.

If you don't invest in your health, you will pay.

"I don't have the money to get health checks done. There's no way I can afford to see a naturopath." Is this you? Let me tell you something: if you don't invest in your health, you will pay. Today I invest more in my physical health than in anything else because my body is the only vessel I have. It's got to last me my whole life and I want my quality of life to be great.

Yes, I understand, you might be struggling to pay bills right now. But have you ever run late on a bill, then somehow managed to pay it? Money will come through for you when you need it, and manifesting money to get important things done is a topic we will cover in Foundation 5: Financial. The older you get, the more important it is to incorporate wellness items into your budget as investments in your health. These might include purchasing high-quality vitamins and setting an alarm daily so you actually remember to take them, and having full health checks annually with your doctor and gynaecologist, as well as investing in good food for your body.

Something I've started investing in is NAD+, a supplement that can reduce and even reverse your body's symptoms of ageing, including cognitive functioning. I've read up on it and listened to podcasts about it: NAD (nicotinamide adenine dinucleotide) is a co-enzyme required by every living cell in your body to help generate energy. As you get older, your levels of this co-enzyme fall, which is why you start forgetting things and feeling less energetic. The product isn't cheap but if you had the choice would you rather spend $2,000 on your health or a Gucci bag? Think about it.

Foundation 1: Physical

If you don't pay for your health now, you'll pay for it later. Some people work themselves into the ground, only to try to repair their broken health later with the money they've made. Whether you go down this route or start prioritising your health now is a decision you'll have to make for yourself. I can't make it for you.

Investing in your health could mean doing anything from ten minutes of star-jumps to two hours of gym a day. I'm not saying to only do ten minutes; likewise, I'm not saying to do two hours. This is my advice: wherever you're at right now, just add a little bit more to see how you will feel. My aim in this chapter is to encourage you to improve your health by minute improvements. If you're already doing two hours a day at the gym, perhaps it's time to look into drinking more water? If you're already drinking your daily quota of water for good health, try to improve your quality of sleep. If quality of sleep is something you already have sorted, then consider exploring ways of investing money in your health: say, by taking supplements or visiting a nutritionist or naturopath. Many people don't believe in wellness doctors, but they've been crucial in my health journey: naturopaths can help you assess your health in a holistic way and find solutions for your individual body's issues.

Of course, I understand that some of these steps require money – an appointment with a naturopath, for example, or having a blood test to see which vitamins you need or whether your hormone levels are optimal. And if you're a mother, you might be thinking, "Oh, but I don't have enough money or time to do any of this."

Feeling that you don't have the resources for such interventions is fine; this is a decision that you will have to make yourself. For me, my physical health is a priority, because if I don't invest enough in my body, then nothing else works. So even though I haven't been

Good Girl

to the gym in a while, I'm still practising other ways to support my body. Something you can do for your health which won't cost you a thing is to track your daily habits: what food do you consume in a day, for example? Today, your Physical Foundation goal could be to keep track of what you've eaten and how your body reacts to certain foods.

I can't exactly remember the last time I was at the gym. Was it two months ago? Three? I dip my toe in and out, but I know that I'm currently neglecting my physical health a bit. That said, I have my other healthy practices in place: I usually walk 10,000 steps a day, 7,000 at the very least; I take my vitamins, I take my NAD+ supplements, I have quality of sleep and I drink plenty of water, so I have invested plenty in my physical health.

You are the only one with the power to change your life. And now is the time to do it – otherwise, when? Instead of thinking, "One day I'll do this," think of today as Day One. We'll make a commitment together to start the process. Yes, it's hard to confront your internal programming, which is why most people avoid doing this work. Tackling the physical – going for a walk or starting a gym membership – is much easier than challenging the thought loops in your head. But it has to be done. And it's about taking little steps, every single day. Onward.

Foundation 2: Mental & emotional

To level up in life, you have to level up in your brain.

Standing where I am now, I know that life can be amazing. But if you're in a hole, how do you get from there to here? Your brain is a computer – so are you running it on outdated software? Maybe it's time for an upgrade!

The answer is that you have to change your mind, your belief system, your outlook in life, the way you think of yourself and the world around you, but most importantly you need to upgrade the blueprint of your life. What's a blueprint? A blueprint is a map your mind turns to when you look for answers – it is a combination of your past experiences, conclusions you have made, what your environment has taught you, and so on. Your blueprint deeply and secretly drives all your decisions – from small details like the clothes you choose to wear to bigger decisions, like who you might marry.

For example, you may work in an environment where bright red lipstick is required but you don't want to wear it. But it's the norm – every woman must wear it and everywhere you look you see red lipstick. You might question the manager about it, but you are told it's simply the way it is. Then, when you change jobs,

Good Girl

you face the same expectations. After some time facing the constant visual reinforcement of all other women wearing bright red lipstick, added to the verbal reinforcement from your manager and the unquestioning attitude of everyone else who sees it as "normal" and isn't bothered by it, you will end up accepting it as it is. And soon, even if you hate red lipstick yourself, it will become your norm also.

The same applies to larger life-choices like choosing a husband. If you have always dated men who are dominant and often make all the decisions, and that is what your parents were like, as well as most other relationships around you, this will be all you know of what marriage can look like. Without realising it, you have adopted a blueprint that this is the "norm" and you will not see any issues with marrying someone who is dominant and makes all the decisions. Your environment and your experience, as well as your interpretation of those experiences, have all shaped you. They have created a blueprint for you, without you even knowing it.

Imagine this scenario. I was born in Cambodia, so my primary language is Khmer/Cambodian. You might have been born in Australia, so naturally you speak English. Our environments have shaped the very tongue in which we speak. I could speak English somewhat fluently at the age of seventeen, after a year of vigorous learning. Now, picture me with this limiting belief: "You are Cambodian so you shouldn't learn English." Picture me growing up with no access to MTV or the Cartoon Network, with the entire population in my country hating the English language. Imagine my parents drilling into me that "English is an evil language which no one should learn." If I went to school and the teacher and my classmates all said the same, what do you think my belief would be about the English language? Would I learn it? What would

Foundation 2: Mental & emotional

then form my belief system? Would I watch any movies in English? What would my blueprint be? Would I marry someone whose native tongue is English? I'm not claiming that either Khmer or English is better or worse than each other – that's not the point here. They are just languages. Whilst this is an obviously extreme example, it demonstrates how our environment and perception can unknowingly shape our belief system and create a blueprint that doesn't serve us.

The good news is that, just like a computer we can change the program and upgrade or delete it as we see fit. The way we think can then be changed by changing the blueprint stamped on us by our environment. When we change our thoughts, we change how we feel. And when we change our feelings, we change our motivation. When we change our motivation, we change our actions. And ultimately, when we change our actions, we alter the outcome. Major shifts start within, not from somewhere "out there". Change starts in *us*, with what we really want in life. And for many people, this is the key question: *what do I want?*

If you don't know the answer to this question – and many people don't – how can you find out what you want? Maybe it's about spending time with yourself, befriending yourself, starting to love yourself, getting to know yourself. Some people know very little about themselves; they struggle to be alone, because solitude can be scary. If you ask, "What is your end goal? Where do you want to go in life?", often they can't tell you. Because they're so stuck where they are, they can't imagine anything different. Or they want what other people want or have, and essentially end up chasing someone else's dreams rather than their own. So, much of the work on this journey is about expanding our thinking. It's about imagining that something you dream of is actually possible.

Good Girl

Our brains are computers, ceaselessly taking in information from our surroundings. As we go about our day, we take pictures and videos with our eyes and record audio with our ears, and the files get stored in our brains. Here's the problem: if these files are attached to a strong emotion, they will yield a particular type of narrative – one which is not necessarily the truth. These narratives take up storage space in our head and are simply the product of our environment. Like any machine, the brain requires maintenance. We need to update our systems and upgrade our software regularly, because if we keep running the same software over and over, we will keep getting the same result. To level up in life, you have to level up in your brain.

Becoming more aware of the brain's functions and your particular thought patterns and narratives can help you manage your emotions – and your life – better. Everyone is smart enough for this. Unless you have a diagnosis from a doctor that you are not intelligent, this is merely a limiting belief that needs to be immediately eradicated. There's no such thing as not being smart enough to receive new information or being too old to learn anything new. The only way forward is to feed your brain properly.

When I moved from Cambodia to Australia at the age of 20, I believed I spoke fluent English. However, the kind of English spoken in Australia was a little different, so I had no confidence speaking English here because I thought I wasn't smart enough. Today, I look at myself and think, "Wow, I can speak four languages! How many people do I know who can do that?" For the record, I speak Cambodian, Thai, English and Teochew, a dialect of Chinese which is my mother's native language. By reminding myself of this, I give myself confidence. I keep telling myself, "You know what, Piyané, you *are* smart."

Foundation 2: Mental & emotional

Telling you I'm smart is not about bragging; I work hard on my knowledge, and I recognise the person I have become today. The key is accepting that we are smart and that there's nothing wrong with us as people; it's our conditioning and daily habits that may have led us to believe we are not smart enough. Something I'll freely admit is that I didn't handle my own taxes until I was about 30 because I didn't understand anything about it. I felt intimidated by conversations about tax, investments and finance in general, and I'd get nervous when I had to set up a company and hire people more knowledgeable than I was, because I feared it might expose me when I couldn't follow what they were talking about! Nowadays I intentionally seek out people who know more than I do. I acknowledge that I'm just one person with one brain, one pair of eyes and one pair of ears. I can't hear and see everything, so I need other brains to optimise my performance. Since I'm not good with numbers, I employ both a tax accountant and a bookkeeper – professionals who have graduated from university, with many years of experience in accounting and tax, and who are excellent at their jobs. I can confidently hand over my tax work to them.

Confidence is built from repetition. *I am smart. I am smart.* This is part of the affirmation I repeated daily for a couple of years. In the beginning I felt like a fraud because I didn't believe it. But when you repeat something enough, your brain will start looking for proof that it exists. If I mention the word "green" and you look around the room, all you will notice is green. You won't see all the red, purple or pink, because your brain is not looking for those colours, only for green. It's exactly the same with affirmations: when I repeated that I was smart, I would start looking for evidence for it throughout the day. I answered emails in a professional way I hadn't thought possible. I was able to solve

Good Girl

problems I didn't expect to. When I learned something new that I didn't think I capable of, it supported my statement "I am smart."

Talent takes you only half of the way. If you have talent but don't repeatedly use it, your talent is as good as useless. Taking action and practising a skill are far more important than just being born with a talent. Do you know that right now there are plenty of people out there who are far less qualified than you, doing the things you want to do? They're just trying to figure it out as they go along. They don't have all the knowledge – nobody does – but that hasn't stopped them. What's stopping you?

I'm no doctor and I can't cure your depression, but I have battled depression for more than fifteen years, survived the experiences and successfully eradicated the major symptoms, and can now manage the more minor ones. And this is what I have learned: you don't just wake up one day in a state of depression. You don't go from "I'm happy, I love my life, I love myself, things are amazing" to falling into a pit of sadness. Depression happens as a result of events and thought patterns that lead to it: such as low self-esteem, beating yourself up, and feeling you're not good enough. Consider babies: they don't have low self-esteem. Nothing scares them. They'll reach for anything, try anything, touch anything – electrical sockets, a visitor's hair – just ask a mother! Low self-esteem is *taught* and *learned*. Over the course of your life, people have beaten you down and, unfortunately, you've believed them, because when something is repeated often enough, we believe it.

Whose voice tells you that you're not good enough? Surely it's not yours; you were merely trained to think that way. Imagine having grown up in a nourishing environment where you were rewarded for simply being yourself. Imagine not having to achieve straight As to receive praise, and imagine your parents

Foundation 2: Mental & emotional

expressing sentiments like, "I love you for who you are. I'll give you honest criticism when I think you could do better, but I love you, however you are right now. You do not have to do anything to earn my love; you don't have to look a certain way or achieve particular grades. My love is always there for you." Perhaps you did grow up in an environment like that, but many of us didn't. Imagine feeling free to tell your parents, "I want to be a singer" (or artist or designer), and instead of them saying, "I don't think you can sing/paint/design. I doubt you'll make it. I don't think there's a career in that. Think again – become a lawyer instead", they encourage you daily to pursue your dreams and show you that they have your back. They come to all your auditions, supporting and applauding you – and here's the best part: when you screw up, they love you just the same.

Most people with low self-esteem have grown up without that kind of support. If that's your experience, you probably have internal software running that's no longer serving you well. It was installed by someone else and now it's well out of date. For you to take any new information in, you need to uninstall, or unlearn, certain parts of your thinking.

I'm not a brain expert; I'm just someone who reads a lot, attends seminars and learns from other people. Yet all those mind hacks won't make a difference if you don't change your lifestyle. If your surroundings are negative – you're scrolling on your phone constantly, gossiping with your friends, constantly hearing pessimistic news – your brain will run on negativity which isn't even real. We *are* our environment. Our surroundings should nourish us, not stress us, and we have control over some of this. Consider how many of us start scrolling through social media the moment we go to the toilet or when we're casually sitting on the couch or when we have a moment to ourselves in the car. It gives us a quick hit of dopamine but can become addictive and eat up our time. Choose again.

To improve the quality of what goes into your brain, look to books. You can learn a lot very quickly by reading. I've read 228 books in seven years, many of them as audio books. This is not to brag. To be honest it is a bit excessive. I just want to show you how determined I've been in my quest to develop myself and upgrade my software so I can function on the same level of the people I admire and aspire to be like. When I started my journey to heal myself and improve my life, I became a consumer of informative books. I was like a sponge, reading everything I could lay my hands on. I went through a phase for a year and a half where I read a book a week, or a book every five days, sometimes every three days. I immersed myself in learning from these books, easily reading 100 titles over about two years. (I told you I like to dive into things.)

I also like to apply lessons I've learned as I go along, but because I was reading so many books by different experts and teachers, I started getting confused. It was hard to know which of the many tools to apply. Eventually I stopped my reading binge, and now I'm over that phase of consuming information avidly; in the past six months I've probably only read three or four books. Now it's all about distilling what I've learned, applying it to my life, and sharing it with you.

Books that rewired my mind

- *Awaken the Giant Within: How to Take Immediate Control of Your Mental, Emotional, Physical and Financial Destiny!*

Foundation 2: Mental & emotional

by Tony Robbins.[12] Tony transformed my mindset, from that of a weepy little girl who believed she was nothing to that of a woman who knew she was worthy of love. In fact, I am everything I am today because of him. Merely sitting here and breathing, I'm deserving of love. I don't have to dress a certain way or rein my personality in; I have a right to be loved for who I am. I deserve love from my friends when I'm feeling down and I don't have to feel like a burden to them. I can give myself a mental health day off work when I need it because I deserve that love from myself. I have a new sense of self-confidence. Tony is behind all of this. Although I recommend any title written by him, this book is a great starting point.

- *The Four Agreements: A Practical Guide to Personal Freedom* by Don Miguel Ruiz.[13] One of the agreements, "Be impeccable with your word", is key to the journalling task from Foundation 1: setting intentions for the day and following through. Being impeccable with your word towards yourself is how you build self-respect and better boundaries.

- *Girl, Wash Your Face: Stop Believing the Lies about Who You Are So You Can Become Who You Were Meant to Be* by Rachel Hollis.[14] Written in a very relatable way, this was

---

12 Tony Robbins, *Awaken the Giant Within: How to Take Immediate Control of Your Mental, Emotional, Physical and Financial Destiny!* (Free Press: 1992).

13 Don Miguel Ruiz, *The Four Agreements: A Practical Guide to Personal Freedom* (Amber Allen: 2011).

14 Rachel Hollis, *Girl, Wash Your Face: Stop Believing the Lies about Who You Are So You Can Become Who You Were Meant to Be* (Thomas Nelson: 2018).

one of the first self-help books I ever read. It provoked a huge emotional reaction in me and inspired me to go deeper into self-development.

- *You are a Badass: How to Stop Doubting Your Greatness and Start Living an Awesome Life* by Jen Sincero.[15] This changed my mindset and primed me to read other self-development books.
- *The Power of Now: A Guide to Spiritual Enlightenment* by Eckhart Tolle.[16] This is the first spiritual self-help book I read. It taught me how to be in the "now". Depression comes from the past and anxiety comes from our anticipation of the future, but we often distract ourselves from the present moment by, say, scrolling on our phones. We're scared of the present and the thoughts and feelings that might arise given half a chance, which is why it's worth giving meditation a go.
- *Breaking The Habit of Being Yourself: How to Lose Your Mind and Create a New One*[17] and *Becoming Supernatural: How Common People Are Doing the Uncommon* by Dr Joe Dispenza.[18] *Becoming Supernatural* changed my thinking about manifestation and creating what I dreamed of. It can help you manifest the body, business and life you

---

15 *You are a Badass: How to Stop Doubting Your Greatness and Start Living an Awesome Life* by Jen Sincero (Running Press: 2013).

16 Eckhart Tolle, *The Power of Now: A Guide to Spiritual Enlightenment* (Hodder Paperbacks: 2001)

17 Dr Joe Dispenza, *Breaking The Habit of Being Yourself: How to Lose Your Mind and Create a New One* (Hay House: 2012).

18 Dr Joe Dispenza, *Becoming Supernatural: How Common People Are Doing the Uncommon* (Hay House: 2017).

Foundation 2: Mental & emotional

want.
- *What Happened to You?: Conversations on Trauma, Resilience, and Healing* by Oprah Winfrey and Bruce D. Perry.[19] This explained so much to me about healing the younger self.
- *The Gifts of Imperfection*[20] and *Daring Greatly: How the Courage to Be Vulnerable Transforms the Way We Live, Love, Parent, and Lead* by Brené Brown.[21] Her research and thinking have opened up healthy conversations about shame and courage.
- *Atomic Habits: An Easy & Proven Way to Build Good Habits & Break Bad Ones* by James Clear.[22] You won't necessarily be able to change all your habits, but what you can do is attach new habits to your old ones. For example, I like to sleep in but then I catch up on my emails in bed! Thank you, James.
- *The 7 Habits of Highly Effective People* by Stephen Covey.[23] A classic for the experienced self-help reader.

---

19 Oprah Winfrey and Bruce D. Perry, *What Happened to You?: Conversations on Trauma, Resilience, and Healing* (Bluebird: 2021).

20 Brené Brown, *The Gifts of Imperfection Let Go of Who You Think You're Supposed to Be and Embrace Who You Are* (Hazelden Publishing: 2010).

21 Brené Brown, *Daring Greatly: How the Courage to Be Vulnerable Transforms the Way We Live, Love, Parent, and Lead* (Portfolio: 2013).

22 James Clear, *Atomic Habits: An Easy & Proven Way to Build Good Habits & Break Bad Ones* (Penguin: 2018).

23 Stephen R. Covey *The 7 Habits of Highly Effective People*, (Simon and Schuster: 1998).

TIPS AND TOOLS

- **List your Mental & Emotional goal for the day** in your journal. To meditate for five minutes? To just sit in silence for five minutes? If you're a mother, maybe your goal will be to allow a longer time to poop – five whole minutes, with no kid in the bathroom! Maybe your goal reads, "Today I'm going to spend ten minutes reading and aim to read six pages" or "Today I'm going to watch a TED Talk."
- **Take care of your mind for ten minutes daily.** This could be anything from reading to listening to a stimulating podcast or having an interesting conversation with someone. After only ten minutes you'll feel aligned with life again. Self-development books are my go-to for mental nourishment, but if reading isn't your thing, listen to audiobooks, find recommended podcasts, talks and YouTube channels to stimulate your mind, or attend a seminar on a topic you're curious about. Educate yourself, especially in areas where you're trying to improve your functioning. This is important if you're struggling with depression, low self-esteem or other mental health issues.
- **Snap out of unhelpful thoughts.** Our emotions are often driven by our thoughts, and these thoughts can be changed. We have the power to choose better thoughts: you can learn how move from one thought to another quickly, rather than dwelling on a certain unhelpful thought. Try placing an elastic band around your wrist for a few days, and whenever you catch yourself thinking something negative about yourself or your life, snap the band and choose a better thought. This will make you more aware of your inner monologue and help you

Foundation 2: Mental & emotional

transition to more positive, encouraging thoughts.

- **Eat brain food.** The right fuel can help your brain become healthier, sharper and less foggy. If you're coming out of an abusive relationship or another traumatic situation, your brain will be in fight-or-flight mode and your memory and cognitive functioning may be impaired.

   Six years ago, when I was recovering from depression, I'd walk into a room and ask myself, "Why am I here? What am I doing?" It wasn't that I was getting older and my memory wasn't so sharp any more; if you've been through trauma and been stuck in survival mode for a long time, your nervous system will have become dysregulated. Your brain's neural pathways won't function normally and it can take a few years for your nervous system to become regulated again and for your adrenal glands to recover from fatigue. If you feel you're not taking in new information optimally, certain foods can help. A healthy diet rich in fruit, vegetables and wholegrains, and low in saturated fat and sugar, can work to protect your brain's networks. Try these specific foods to improve your brain functioning:

   » Oily fish, including salmon, mackerel, tuna, herring and sardines
   » Dark chocolate (yay!), with at least 70 percent cocoa
   » Berries, particularly strawberries, blackberries, blueberries, blackcurrants and mulberries
   » Nuts and seeds, including sunflower seeds, flaxseed almonds and hazelnuts
   » Coffee (just don't overdo it)
   » Avocados

Good Girl

- » Eggs
- » Peanuts
- » Soya beans and soya products
- » Broccoli
- » Leafy greens, such as kale
- » Wholegrains such as brown rice, oats, barley, bulgur wheat, whole-grain bread and wholewheat pasta.

- **Step outside your comfort zone.** You'll need a new set of skills to get to the next level, so sign up for that online course you've been eyeing off, join that group for monthly meet-ups, or strike up a conversation with that interesting person. Be willing to feel a bit uncomfortable while your life shapeshifts.
- **Romanticise your life.** I romanticise my life every single day. I meditate on it, and it makes me think, "Oh my god, my life is amazing!" People might think that's a bit self-absorbed, but it's not. Why can't I say that my life is amazing? I'm sure there are plenty of people out there who have better lives than what society wants for them. For example, I love spearfishing, diving and having underwater adventures in nature. To me, that's amazing. But other people ask, "Piyané, why are you doing that?" So, the important thing is to draw from the experience of what's amazing for *you*. And what if you really don't feel there's anything to romanticise about in your life? Utilise your brain's power each day by imagining yourself doing things that you do think are amazing. When you start mentally placing yourself in situations, you're far more likely to place yourself there in real life.
- **Accept compliments.** Here's a test of self-esteem: how do

Foundation 2: Mental & emotional

you take a compliment? Is your immediate reaction to feel proud or to instantly reject the notion? Today, I'm asking you to give yourself the credit. Say thank you when you are praised. Give yourself a pat on the back. Who else is going to do it for you?

- **Use positive self-talk.** Affirmations are a method of retraining the brain. You might wonder, "Will it work to look in the mirror and tell myself something I don't believe, such as: *I look beautiful today. I am smart. I am beautiful. I am courageous.*"? Yes, it will. Repeat these affirmations often enough and you will eventually believe them. These are my mantras, by the way, and I've taught them to my daughter. Before she goes to bed each night, we recite together, "I am beautiful. I am smart. I am courageous. I am joy. I am fun. And I love myself." We put our hands on our hearts when we say this. Repetition is the goal, and here's why: one day, when you're feeling down, when your boss or sister-in-law or someone else has told you you're not good enough, or that you shouldn't be doing X or Y, you'll have this to fall back on. With enough training and repetition, these affirmations will become your default thinking. When you rely on external forces for validation, your day will be affected by what other people do or say to you. But if you have a strong internal system, you'll be far less affected by what's happening on the outside. Be warned: elevating your mindset will feel foreign in the beginning. At first you won't believe the affirmations. Of course not! If you've been believing you're not good enough for ten years, why would you believe me if I suddenly told you that you were? Give yourself time to acclimatise. Remember, your brain is an incredibly powerful tool. Nobody can install new software for you. *You* have to do that yourself.

- **Unlearn your limiting beliefs.** On a piece of paper, write down the harshest things you regularly think about yourself, those critical statements your brain has running on a loop. "I'm not pretty enough", "I have fat arms", "One of my breasts is weirdly bigger than the other", "I'm not smart enough", "I'm not equal to men", "I'm not white enough". List all the statements you can dredge up, then sit back and look at them. Imagine someone you love is walking around with these messages running through their mind. What would that do to them? And what is it doing to you?

Now, on another piece of paper, let's change each negative statement to something far more pleasing. Write statements that you resonate with – if you're short, don't write down "I am tall", for example. To replace "I'm not smart enough", you could write, "I have the ability to learn. I don't know X yet, but I can find out the answer." You might change "I'm not pretty enough; I'm fat" to "I'm not the weight I want to be, but I can work towards looking the way I want to look." And consider adding, "Who defines what is beautiful anyway? Maybe I *am* beautiful." If you ask me, you are beautiful because you were created this way. As for the parts you want to change, do what you need to. I'm not against plastic surgery: if you have the means and you want to do it, go for it. If not, then make peace with that part of yourself.

These are merely suggestions. Find the language that sits well with you, so that you feel good when you read your updated statements.

I used to think, "I'm not smart enough. I'm not skinny enough.

I'm not white enough." I changed that first statement to "I am smart" and wrote it every day and repeated it to myself, and I felt like an idiot for doing so. Saying I was smart was a lie, right? But that's just an example of my old programming trying to get at me. The ego, terrified of dying, tries to get its hooks into any evidence that you're moving on with your life and drag you back into the past. But repeat your new statements often and long enough, and you will find new evidence to support them. For example, when you solve a problem for yourself or your boss or a friend, you'll think, "Ah, I did that!" and this little win will support your claim.

In my opinion and from my reading in this area, this is how you form your self-belief. This will then create your view about yourself – and this is displayed in all areas of your life. So let's be honest here. Let's write down your "I AM" statement, the lies you believe about yourself on one side of the paper like below. On the other side write down the truth, your truth.

Dive deep into your identity

- **Write a letter to your younger self.** To change the way you think, you will need to delve into your early programming. Your relationship with your younger self has a huge influence on your mental health. Think of the earliest traumatic incident you can recall, the first time you thought, "I'm not good enough". Did a moment pop up in your head? Now let's write a letter to your younger self in which you thank her, give her grace and give her the credit and praise she deserves. Because of what was said or done to her by parents, teachers or others in her community, she didn't feel good enough – but she kept going, for you. You are here today because of that little girl. Let's heal from there.

At the top of a piece of paper, write, "Dear little [your name], age X". Then write a letter in which you honour her. What is it that you want to thank her for? What is it that you're sorry about? What is it that she witnessed or heard or experienced that you wish you had the power to protect her from? If you could see that little girl right now, going through what she did, how would you protect her? Tell her that she is safe now and that it's okay for her to be a child again. She does not have to carry the weight of the world on her shoulders. You are able to take over from now on.

Next, do this work on each negative event that comes to mind, where part of you is stuck at a particular age because of something you experienced. We have different phases in life – perhaps you were a shy girl who played with Barbies at age six, and at ten you were a bit of a tomboy rebel. Which stage of your younger self have you felt trapped in? When did your younger self feel naughty simply for expressing her thoughts, using her voice and stepping out of the norm, for example? Write as many letters as you can – let's aim for ten. Start with the earliest traumatic experience, then write a letter to yourself at each subsequent experience. The first letter, however, is the most important, so write this letter as passionately as you can. And remember, you're not doing this alone, you're doing it with me. We're confronting your scary thoughts together.

Now that you've written down your limiting beliefs, you'll start noticing how much the thoughts that run through your mind each day affect your life. If your girlfriends are gossiping about

Foundation 2: Mental & emotional

someone you know (even thinking about this makes my brain cells die a little), you'll walk away with your brain primed to focus on outfits, fake tan or whatever you've been discussing. And it will be on the lookout for more gossip. It is crucial what you feed your brain.

Who "am" I?

When you do something for long enough, it becomes a habit, and eventually it becomes your identity. "I failed" becomes "I'm a failure", for example. An action becomes an identity, and an identity is hard to reverse. When you've done something wrong, it's easy to forgive yourself; when someone else does something wrong, it's easy to forgive them. Say your husband forgot to buy milk for the house; it's easy to forgive him. So what if he forgot the milk today? He's human and made a mistake. He might say, "Oh honey, I forgot. I'm sorry," and your heart will soften immediately. But when he does it regularly, over time it becomes his identity: he is unreliable. And it's not about the milk any more. Do something for long enough and an identity becomes attached to it.

What identity don't you like about yourself? "I'm lazy", "I'm unreliable", "I'm stupid", "I'm ugly"? Let's change the "I am's" and challenge these beliefs. The root cause of many of our mental issues is the belief that "I'm not good enough". But why is it important that you be "good enough"? If you're home alone in your pyjamas, there's no need to wear make-up or do your hair or be any particular way. Who do you want to be "good enough" for? We want to be good enough because *we want to be loved*. It's the human condition.

What makes you believe you're not good enough? Let's find proof. Write down a few points next to each statement. When I was starting my self-development journey, I thought this exercise

Good Girl

was stupid and felt a lot of resistance towards it. I wanted a quick fix – just give me a pill! I didn't want to write all these unpleasant things down. How was this going to help me anyway?

Trust the process. It *does* help. Because we're community animals, a sense of love and belonging makes us happy. We need it. Lack of love equals exclusion, which can feel life-threatening, because during our evolutionary history being excluded from the group could be extremely dangerous. Ask anyone who's lying on their deathbed for their last thoughts, and it'll never be, "I wish I'd changed those hideous curtains in the living room", or "I wish I'd spent more hours at the office and worked harder." Never. It's always something like, "Please tell my sister I love her" or "I wish I'd told my father I loved him more often." Love is the core of our existence.

Other animals are born with defence systems, wired to feed themselves. Human babies, however, can't fend for themselves without love: they live off their parents for at least eighteen years! For the first ten years, parents' love ensures their offspring's survival. As children, we are hard-wired to seek love from our caretakers, because without it we'll die. And when we repeatedly have to do certain things to earn that love, or aren't rewarded with the love we need, "I am not good enough" will be engraved on our internal system.

Be aware of the voices in your head and where they come from. Your first instinct as a child wasn't to think, "I'm fat". What happened was that someone told you that you were fat, and you believed it. I know the word "fat" is triggering for many people and, for the record, I have nothing against high body weight. I find everyone beautiful. Yet often we're so stuck in self-criticism that we can't see our own beauty. A woman might walk into a meeting with me and say, "Oh my god, my hair looks so stupid

Foundation 2: Mental & emotional

today", when, actually, that wasn't what I noticed about her at all. I noticed her smile, her energy and her bright red jacket.

This is what we need to undo, starting now. Bear in mind that we're not talking about a one-day habit; if you're 20, 25, 35, 45 years of age, that's how long a habit you need to undo. It took me a few committed years to extricate myself from my old mindset. It's a long road, but I am proof that it can be done.

One day I decided, "That's it, I've had enough of my own bullshit. Look at all these people out there, succeeding in life, doing what I want to do, and they don't know much – I know them! – so how can they be so successful? I'm going to read this self-development book and try the tools because I have nothing to lose. If it doesn't help, I can always go back to being depressed." That was my mindset at the time.

If you don't have faith in this process, you can use my faith. Borrow it for a second; I'll happily lend it to you. I believe in this process completely and I believe you can get there. Think of me as someone who's walking with you through a dark tunnel. I sprint to the end of the tunnel, then run back excitedly to tell you about the light: "Come on, let's go, you're going to love it!"

So... borrow my faith. I've been where you are, and I have seen the light at the end of tunnel. You haven't seen it yet, so I'm here to tell you that it's beautiful. I was once in your place: I didn't think I was beautiful or smart enough or could do most of the things I'm doing now. If you'd told me back then, when I was depressed and drinking cough syrup to escape the pain, that I'd be on the cover of *Prestige* magazine in a few years, I wouldn't have believed you. If you'd told that bed-ridden girl who wasn't even showering or brushing her teeth for days at a time that she would have her own cosmetics brand, and that her products would be featured in *Marie Claire* and *InStyle* magazines, and that she'd be travelling the world and attending Fashion Weeks and meeting amazing people, she would have scoffed and said, "Yeah, whatever."

I'm here to tell you that it's all possible. Everything you can imagine. And it started the moment I said to myself, "I have officially had enough of my own bullshit."

That's why you need to write all your bullshit down. "I'm not good enough because I'm not smart." Is it true? Or is it true that you just haven't learned about a particular subject yet? Write that down too, next to the other statements. If you're like me and not good with numbers, you can always hire someone to help you with your finances. You don't need a top-notch professional; if you can't pay the full fees, hire a tax practitioner for an hour's consultation to teach you how to do your taxes. Or, if you don't have the money, look for help on YouTube. Write all this down.

Be aware of the long list of excuses we haul out when we don't want to get off our butts and make a change. I *know* you want to have a better life. I *know* you don't want to be depressed. You don't want to be sitting here wondering what you did wrong to end up in this rut where nothing goes your way, where you're barely making ends meet, and where you're not physically where you want to be.

Stop with the excuses. Start with a single moment. When adopting a new mentality, the first step is to be aware of your thoughts throughout the day. When you have a negative thought, pull out your phone, challenge that thought and type a note. Or just pause and observe it. Consider how unfair it is to burden yourself with these self-critical thoughts. To the mothers out there, imagine your beloved son or daughter walking around with this list of negative statements in their head and repeating it over and over to themselves each day. You are someone's daughter,

Foundation 2: Mental & emotional

and if your mother didn't give you the love you needed, I'm here to give it to you. I'm here to tell you that you are good enough, that you are more than worthy of love, and that you can do it. You can start over again: you can reinvent and replace what's in your head with positive affirmations. But you must decide to make the change; I cannot do that for you.

Something else to consider is that if you keep repeating these thoughts, you'll inevitably pass them on to your children. They observe how you live – the way you talk *to* other people, the way you talk *about* other people, the way you talk to and treat *yourself* – and they copy it. You're their role model. So, let's re-parent ourselves and be the generational curse-stoppers. First, do it for yourself and later pay it forward – for a friend or someone else who also needs re-parenting.

That said, although you'll undoubtedly have light-bulb moments on this journey where you think, "Aha, let me re-parent my mother! Let me re-condition my friend! It really helped me!", don't be surprised if they aren't quite as excited as you are. In fact, they might be completely resistant to it.

There's nothing wrong with starting your healing journey alone. You do not need to do this with your best friend, your sister or brother, with your mother or partner. It starts with you. In fact, I highly encourage you to do this by yourself. Don't involve other people in this process because it's extremely personal, and you need the freedom to be as raw and real as possible while you transform.

The following pages include worksheets to help you with these reflections, or download them from **www.piyane.com/resources**.

Good Girl

Lies I tell myself:

I am dumb

I am ugly

I am a woman

I am a failure

I am a burden

Good Girl

Ultimate truths:

I am smart. I just need to learn the skills.

I am so beautiful

I am just as capable as men.
How others view me based on my gender isn't my business.

I failed at xxx, but I have learned from it!

I am so loved. I know at least 1 person who wants me to be on this earth

Good Girl

Good news! Your emotions are not permanent.

Let's dive deeper into the world of our feelings. Where does emotion come from? The Latin word for emotion, "emotere", literally means "energy in motion". The most important thing to know is that emotions are temporary, not permanent, and you can feel multiple emotions in a day. This means that if you're feeling sad right now, good news – you're not going to be feeling sad forever.

The key to living the life you dream of is not to let your emotions rule you. The habits of successful people boil down to this: when your mind is stronger than your emotions, you can get things done. I am proof of this – today I function completely differently from that depressed, bed-ridden woman six years ago who was crushed by her own thoughts and emotions.

When I say your mind needs to be stronger than your emotions, I don't mean that your mind must control your emotions. It's not that you need to say, "I'm feeling sad right now but I need to control that sadness so I feel happier." No. We're taught in therapy to sit with our emotions and this is for a good reason. The first step in healing is to *feel* your emotions and know how you feel; it's an essential part of the process and should not be left out. It's good practice to write in a journal to acknowledge how you feel each day. That said, there is a fine balance between needing to feel your emotions and needing to stop. At a certain point, your mind must step in and be the "bigger person" who takes care of your emotions, so that your negative feelings don't take over your life. Switching mode is an important skill: here, you have to be able to switch from that emotional, messy state to your logical mind, to observe how you're feeling and choose your next step.

Let's take an example. Say you've been triggered and are feeling highly emotional. Often these emotions are not responding

Foundation 2: Mental & emotional

to the person who pressed the trigger; your emotional response likely results from a long string of issues you've harboured for years. In fact, the emotions come from your inner child. You might think you're angry at the person in front of you, but actually you're upset about an issue that dates all the way back to your childhood. What can help is reflecting on that formative experience.

Whatever emotion you're feeling when you are triggered, you have felt it in the past. If you are reading this book, you have lived long enough to have experienced the whole gamut of emotions available on this earth. A language barrier might prevent you from naming certain emotions, but you've certainly felt the full range of human feelings.

How do you get in touch with your emotions? How do you become attuned to yourself right now? How do you measure the level of frustration, anger or whatever you're feeling? Because emotion is energy in motion, we have to give ourselves space to feel our emotions. Sit with your feelings and try to identify how you feel. Then, if you sit with that emotion long enough, it will transform. For example, I might be feeling angry because I've just had a fight with my mother, but when I sit and reflect on this anger, I find that it's not actually anger; it is, in fact, grief. I'm grieving the lack of support and love I need from her. My grief is for something that's missing in my life.

Also, the intention of this book is to build a "bad bitch"! I want to build you up so you can succeed and achieve wonderful things, while still feeling your emotions. Whatever reason you have for being emotional is valid. Your feelings are there, whether you like it or not, and they are valid.

How do you handle your emotions? It's fine to express your feelings in ways that don't harm you or others: punching a punch bag or a pillow, screaming, crying, writing your feelings to

Good Girl

someone in a letter you never send, shouting out your feelings when you're alone, for example. Dissociation used to be my main tool for dealing with my emotions. A natural response to trauma for many, dissociation is a mental process of disconnecting from your thoughts, feelings, memories or sense of identity. It's like looking at your life through someone else's eyes: from a zoomed-out view where you see yourself like another person who's going through certain experiences and emotions. As I'm not a psychologist, I highly recommend you speak to a professional or read up on dissociation if this strikes a chord with you. From my experience, it comes in different forms, from an intense distancing from yourself to a dull numbness where you feel apathetic and not yourself. You might be saying, "Sure, no problem" to everything. Dissociation can be so subtle that you no longer identify with the reality in which you're living.

What's your go-to tool for survival? It could be self-medicating, or binge-drinking, or maybe it's being the big party girl or the funny one who's always cracking jokes. Often, people who commit suicide always appeared, to others, to be strong and have everything together. In fact, it's those who don't talk about their emotions who are most vulnerable, particularly men. The suicide rate among males worldwide is higher than that of females: although women have more suicidal thoughts, men follow through and commit suicide more often. Globally, the suicide rate is more than twice as high among men as women. In the Western world, the suicide rate for men is three to four times higher than for women. It's worth finding healthy tools for acknowledging and expressing our emotions.

Climb the ladder of emotions to a better feeling place.

How many emotions are there? Depending on which theory

Foundation 2: Mental & emotional

you follow, there are anything from six basic emotions (sadness, happiness, fear, anger, surprise and disgust) to 34,000 different emotions felt by humans. If you want something in between, researchers at University of California, Berkeley identified these 27 categories of emotion[24], presented here in alphabetical order:

- Admiration
- Adoration
- Aesthetic appreciation
- Amusement
- Anxiety
- Awe
- Awkwardness
- Boredom
- Calmness
- Confusion
- Craving
- Disgust
- Empathic pain
- Entrancement
- Envy
- Excitement
- Fear
- Horror
- Interest

---

24 See Alan S. Cowen and Dacher Keltner, "Self-report captures 27 distinct categories of emotion bridged by continuous gradients", September 2017, https://www.pnas.org/doi/abs/10.1073/pnas.1702247114.

Good Girl

- Joy
- Nostalgia
- Romance
- Sadness
- Satisfaction
- Sexual desire
- Sympathy
- Triumph

We will all experience these different emotions to a certain degree. The question is: how do you shift your emotional state if it's causing you suffering? Let's face it, you're probably not reading my book because you're the most amazingly content, highest-achieving person you know you can be right now. No judgement: I'm on this journey with you, remember. In fact, as I'm writing this section on emotions today, I'm not in a very good place myself, and that's because I'm arguing with someone I love very much, someone with whom I would rather not be fighting. Fighting is something we people-pleasers avoid, as we don't like confrontation. As "good girls", we don't want to come across as aggressive and nasty. That's why we have these outbursts – because we've been holding onto what's bothering us, it's built up and now it's been shaken up and *boom!* Suddenly there's Coca-Cola everywhere!

I don't know what you're feeling right this moment, but let's say that your emotional state could be described as "shit". The good news is that a hierarchy of emotions exists, a ladder you can climb, step by step, to get to a better place. There are various versions of this hierarchy, but here's one based on the book *Power*

Foundation 2: Mental & emotional

vs Force by David R. Hawkins:[25]

- Shame
- Guilt
- Apathy
- Grief
- Fear
- Craving/desire
- Anger
- Pride
- Courage
- Neutrality
- Willingness
- Acceptance
- Reason (thinking clearly and rationally)
- Love
- Joy
- Peace
- Enlightenment

Your emotions set the tone for your day, your week and your life. And your thoughts and feelings are intertwined: you have a thought, then an emotion is attached to it. Or you might feel an emotion, then attach a thought to it. If you place emotion above everything else – say, you set your tone for the day as "pissed off with X" for doing what you told them not to do, or not doing what you asked them to do – then you're likely to feel angry

---

25 David R. Hawkins, *Power vs Force: The Hidden Determinates of Human Behavior: The Hidden Determinants of Human Behavior* (Hay House, 2004).

and disappointed for a while. You'll go about your day and start looking for various ways to validate the fact that you are angry and disappointed, and those feelings will multiply. It's similar to when you buy a car and, hey, suddenly everyone's driving the same car! You see cars like yours everywhere. It's how your brain works.

The key is to make intentional decisions to choose thoughts and emotions that serve you better. This is a discipline. If you just wake up and roll the dice regarding your emotions, you'll be like a flag flapping in the wind. This book is important for you as it's here to help you regain a sense of control and learn to regulate your emotions.

I read something recently that resonated with me. In essence, it said that wealth is not measured by the amount of money in our bank accounts, but by the level of regulation of our nervous system. Indeed, I could be the luckiest, happiest woman in the world with all the money I want, but if I get triggered by every little thing, then I'm constantly in survival mode, and where's the freedom in that? I sure as hell can't create anything from that space. The ideal space to inhabit is a beautiful, ever-shifting state that involves surrendering your whole being so that you can create new things. And getting there is something you can learn. Medication, hospitals and retreats have their place, but they can't necessarily heal your nervous system. You have to heal yourself, and this starts with very simple thoughts and actions that set the emotional tone for your whole day. To have a beautiful day, you have to make beautiful decisions, yourself. It's as simple as that.

Aiming to be happy all the time is bullshit.

When moving up the ladder from negativity to positivity, proceed step by step. Don't expect to suddenly jump from feeling desolate

Foundation 2: Mental & emotional

to feeling joyful; that's a huge leap. Merely try to change your current state to something a little more positive. Approach the emotional climb up the ladder incrementally, moving step by step to eventually arrive at an emotional state that is far from where you are now. Every emotion can be useful. Anger is surprisingly close to the emotions we traditionally call "positive" – it can inspire us to take action, for example, which is more productive than feeling apathetic and stuck.

Aiming to be happy all the time is bullshit. Happiness is just an emotion. You feel it for five minutes and then it goes away: someone pisses you off and *poof*, it's gone again. Trying to be constantly happy is toxic positivity at its worst, if you ask me. We cannot possibly achieve permanent happiness, so why aim for that or expect that? I'm not happy all the time; I just regulate my emotions enough that I can go out there and enjoy life, regardless of the emotional state I'm in. It's about the small, incremental actions I take to climb up the emotional ladder towards happiness and joy.

The worst thing is to feel one difficult emotion the whole day, because then you're in a deep pit. I know how hard that is because I was once there: I could be in that pit for two weeks straight, lying in bed, drinking my cough syrup, feeling nothing. That kind of numbness is hard to change, so if you can change your numbness to sadness, crying or anger, that's *good*. You're starting to shift, and you can keep going, keep climbing up the ladder, bit by bit, to a place that feels better. Whatever slightly more positive feeling your emotion changes into is a win. You're not stuck. Let's applaud that!

There's nothing wrong with my experience of the pit of negativity: it served me at the time. But if I had stayed there, I would be so depressed I would have no interest in life. As I've

Good Girl

mentioned, depression is living in the past; anxiety is trying to live in the future. And you're experiencing these sensations because you're not living the life you know you can live. You understand your potential but you're not rising to it. Just keep climbing, step by step, up the emotional ladder, and you will get there.

I wrote earlier that your mind has to be stronger than your emotions – because otherwise, your emotions will drive you to say and do things you're not proud of. Incidentally, words are powerful: you're more likely to lose friendships and relationships over the things you *say* than the things you *do*. You're also most likely to repair relationships with the things you say. If you have a malicious mouth, be careful because it can be destructive. We all lash out at times and say things to hurt others – I know I do – but when we're driven by our emotions and get stuck there, we will also *do* things we later regret. Managing your emotions is crucial: if your mind isn't stronger than your emotions and you keep acting out on your feelings, you will lose, every single time. In contrast, you can be angry at someone but choose not to act. So, let's start creating a healthy adult version of you that is able to control your emotions. By "control" I don't mean not feeling them; I mean containing them. Keep them in a safe space where you can experience and express them without being destructive.

If you're feeling sad right now – maybe someone has hurt your feelings, or your boyfriend has broken up with you or cheated on you, or he's dating someone else and you're feeling jealous of her – let's look at what we can control. We can't control those people! We can't make them come back to us or stop them from dating other women. There's a finite number of things we can control, and other people are not among them. Likewise, we cannot control our environment, but what we can control is *ourselves*. Discipline is the highest form of self-love. You've done

Foundation 2: Mental & emotional

your Physical Foundation, you're doing your Mental & Emotional Foundation, and you've got this far in the book; you're committed to the process and I applaud you for that. You've proved you have discipline.

Now let's go deeper. It's simple to choose better thoughts. Perhaps your go-to method is to distract yourself by hopping onto Netflix, Spotify or a social media platform; maybe you'll read a new snippet about a celebrity getting a divorce and feel a sense of connection with her – but that won't change your emotional state. To change your state, my advice is this: *move*. Go back to the physical. Don't pick up your phone to stalk that guy on social media and scroll yourself into a state; step outside and go for a brisk 30-minute walk or run instead. If you're feeling angry, don't start sending people long essays that you know they won't read. (They'll just skim through it and think, "Oh my god, she's losing her shit again.") We both know this doesn't yield results, so change your actions. Unfortunately, I had a skiing accident and hurt my knee so running isn't a good option for me, but I *can* stretch my body or put on some uplifting music and "shake it off", à la Taylor Swift. It really works. Sure, to someone peering in through the window, you might appear like a crazy, possessed person when you do this, but you have to try to shake off your negative energy physically because it's stored in your body.

Your body, mind and emotions are inextricably linked. Your thoughts are filtered through your emotions, and vice versa, and you feel their energy in your body. You might tell yourself, "I'm feeling flat; I have no energy," but this physical state is being driven by your emotions.

I recommend the book *The Body Keeps the Score: Brain, Mind,*

Good Girl

and Body in the Healing of Trauma by Bessel van der Kolk M.D.[26], which explains how emotions are stored in the body. For example, if you are feeling stressed, your neck and shoulders will feel tense. You'll feel frustration at the base of your neck. And when you have experienced trauma, you often store it in your hips. Listen to your body: a kink in your neck, a cold sore – such ailments can be indicators of your emotions.

MORE TIPS AND TOOLS

How do you stop feeling crappy right now and start feeling better? There are so many ways to get out of your current state, so find one that works for you. If a cold shower is too intense for you, for instance, try writing in a gratitude journal. I heartily invite you to experiment and find the tool will get you out of your negative state – because, although I encourage you to experience your emotion, I'm explicitly telling you not to *stay* there.

- **Do something physical.** First, get moving. Walk. Run. Swim. Stretch. Do yoga. Play table tennis. Try Padel. Put on some music and dance in your living room. You need to work up a sweat.
- **Boost your dopamine levels.** Here are a few ways to boost your levels of the feelgood neurotransmitter, aka "the reward hormone":
  » Getting a good night's sleep
  » Exercising (see above), particularly dancing, swimming and cycling
  » Shopping

---

26 Bessel van der Kolk M.D., *The Body Keeps the Score: Brain, Mind, and Body in the Healing of Trauma* (Penguin, 2015).

Foundation 2: Mental & emotional

- » Having sex
- » Smelling cookies baking in the oven
- » Meditating
- » Listening to music
- » Spending time in nature
- » Eating almonds, bananas, avocados, and eggs – all rich in tyrosine, an amino acid essential for the production of dopamine in the brain

- **Boost your serotonin levels.** Here are hacks to increase the mood-stabilising neurotransmitter:
  - » Smiling, even if you don't feel like it. Faking it works!
  - » Exposure to sunlight
  - » Socialising
  - » Exercising (see above)
  - » Reliving happy memories: go through photos from holidays and events, for example
  - » Taking vitamin D supplements
  - » Having a cold shower or bath
  - » Having a massage
  - » Doing yoga
  - » Mindfulness exercises
  - » A high-fibre diet containing foods rich in amino acid tryptophan: eggs, cheese, salmon, turkey, tofu, nuts, seeds and pineapple.

- **Practise Tony Robbins' morning "Priming" exercise.** It's freely available on YouTube[27]. Spend ten minutes each

---

27 e.g. www.youtube.com/watch?v=faTGTgid8Uc

morning doing this mind exercise guided by him, and you'll start feeling like a new person. Tony's "Priming" combines physical movement – breathing and pumping your arms up and down while seated – with inspiring visualisation. You'll step into moments you feel grateful for, relive moments you feel proud of and grab moments from your future you would like to experience. And you will feel grateful for all you have and excited by the experiences waiting for you.

- **Set a timer and express your emotions in a safe space.** If you're feeling sad, I'm not telling you not to cry. Do cry – but lock the door, set a timer for five or ten minutes, beat the pillow and cry your eyes out. If you're feeling angry, frustrated, disappointed: the same applies. This is important for people-pleasers like us: because we don't often have good boundaries, we might not have a safe space to retreat to. Back in my deep, dark phase, I'd shut myself in closets to feel my emotions because that was the only place I'd feel safe. In an open space I'd feel exposed, which would send me into fight-or-flight mode. If you don't have a room to shut yourself in, go into a bathroom and have a good cry there for five or ten minutes. Have a private space of retreat you can escape to and feel your emotions. But don't stay there. Visit it – but choose not to stay there.

- **Reflect, don't react, when you've been triggered.** Remember, your emotions are heightened by triggers. Afterwards you may feel you overreacted and that the person you lashed out at didn't deserve that response. It pays to take time out and reflect before responding.

Foundation 2: Mental & emotional

- **Write down how you are feeling.** Find five to ten minutes a day where you write down your emotions. This helps your brain order your thoughts and feelings, and often brings you a sense of relief.
- **Write a daily gratitude list: "Three Things I'm Grateful for Today".** Gratitude is the antidote to anxiety. You might tell me you have nothing to be grateful for, that your life is totally shit and your partner and parents are dreadful. That may be true, but there is always something to be grateful for. Always. If you're feeling low and want to get to a better place, practise being grateful every day. The practise rewires your brain: when you know you'll have to write down three things you're grateful for every evening, your mind gets trained to look out for such things. Maybe it's that you have interesting work, or the weather was good, or you got to wake up next to someone you love. Get yourself a nice notebook to use as your daily gratitude journal.

Use one of these tools to get out of your negative state and the rest of your day will be better. And don't just practise one of the tools once a day; take small actions throughout the day to change your mood state and keep it on the up.

You might need to do this when you're in a sticky situation; when your boss is being hard on you, for example. What can you do about it? You can't control this asshole or change his behaviour. You can only change yourself – and choose better actions for yourself. Even if you're busy working towards a deadline and feel you don't have time, you do. Go to the bathroom, take five minutes for yourself and feel your emotions. (Your mental health regulation is more important than this asshole's ego.) In

Good Girl

the bathroom, sort yourself out. What do you need right now? "I need love," you might say. Yes, you need to give yourself love, and you need love from your community too.

First, let's talk about self-love. I learned various tricks from my time in therapy, such as self-soothing: giving myself a hug and stroking my arms, up and down, up and down. I even got a tattoo on my inner arm that says *I love myself*, which I see when I'm soothing myself like this. Looking down while I'm stroking my arms, I see the words tattooed on my arm and it reminds me that I love myself. This helps to get me out of my negative state.

How committed are you to getting out of your state? Here's something that may surprise you: we are addicted to our suffering. It's all we know. If your boss is giving you a hard time, you might meet up with friends for a drink after work and complain the shit out of him. If you keep talking about it, it shows you want to keep the story alive. The story is about your suffering because you're a victim of someone else's actions. I'm not blaming you; those things are real. They have happened to you. But there are two options: you can react to the situation, or you can stop and try something different. Of course, we're all human and we will initially react to our situation. But what's needed is for us to be aware of a pattern of being addicted to the feelings that can keep us locked in.

Have you ever complained to someone about how horrible your boss is, and then they go and tell you how vile *their* boss is, and now you're bonding over your shared suffering? This is not real friendship; this is "trauma-bonding". The two of you are competing over who has the most suffering, who has the best stories to tell about how people have wronged you. You compete by telling your stories – and that's what is keeping your boss (for example) entrenched in the role of aggressor and fanning the

Foundation 2: Mental & emotional

flames of your suffering. This guy is living rent-free in your head! You do not need to keep reliving your horrid experience. Step one is to cut yourself off from gossip and storytelling.

There are two ways to look at situations like this. Firstly, what can I do about it? Can I change this situation? Quit? Go to HR? If so, consider doing it. If not, or it's not possible at the moment, then the second way of looking at it is to accept it without taking it personally. Either way, repeating the story will only keep you stuck and giving your power away.

You probably feel zero compassion for the person who has done you wrong, whether it's your boss, your boyfriend, your husband, your best friend, your sibling, your mother or your father – but when you think about this person, spread a bit of compassion. Why do you think they are behaving the way they are? Happy people don't go around putting people down or trying to ruin their lives. It's likely that this person is suffering, and a sprinkling of compassion can help ease your perspective. Take a step back and tell yourself, "This is actually not personal. What this person is doing is all about them, not me." When I think about the students who bullied me in my twenties, I realise I was a mirror of their personal shame. They were probably ashamed of something in their lives, and their only way of feeling better was to put me down.

Strengthen the adult "you" by exploring your triggers.

I'm sorry if you are going through your own deep, dark phase at the moment. I can understand what that feels like. (And if you aren't down there, I'm glad to hear it!) Choose better actions for yourself today. Take better care of yourself, starting now, because no one else will. We are all adults here, and what we need to do, immediately, is to strengthen the adult "you" so it can look after

Good Girl

the child living inside you, who is stuck in survival mode.

When we are triggered – when we women get called "crazy" for example – all hell can break loose! The person in front of you is not who it's about – I guarantee it. You're feeling two emotions here: firstly, shame. You may think you're feeling anger at being called crazy, for instance, but it's probably shame. Sit with the feeling long enough and you'll remember incidents that might have led people to believe that you did act "crazy" (for the sake of this example). You may have had wild outbursts, jumped to conclusions, or done impetuous things you later regretted. There may be a lot of shame attached to things you've done in the past. And now that you're working on getting better, you aren't resorting to those behaviours any more. So, when this person in front of you uses your trigger word ('crazy') to describe you, you're suddenly furious because you think, "How dare you put me back there! I'm working hard to get away from that! I'm even reading a book about it!"

If you are angry about a string of past events and decisions, let's start by getting out of victimhood. Imagine you've been arguing with someone for half an hour and you're getting nowhere. You aren't resolving the issue because both of you are playing the victim. Now imagine you decide to be the bigger person by owning up to the fact that you made a mistake by judging people: "Honey, I'm very sorry that I said what I said. I'm totally in the wrong." But the other person keeps verbally punching you. You respond, "I'm really sorry. I understand your frustration. If I were you, I'd be angry too." If you are that rock in the dynamic, and you don't let the other person's energy stick on you, it's only a matter of time before they will run out of fight. They can't keep fighting forever with someone who is taking 100 percent responsibility. But the conflict *will* keep going forever if

Foundation 2: Mental & emotional

you play the victim: "Oh yeah? Well, you did X and Y too!" Both of you will annihilate each other.

I'm not saying you should be a punching bag in your relationship. The other person needs to take just as much responsibility for their actions and words when they screw up. This is just an example of how your highest self would have handled the situation.

If you're wanting to grow, you can't be up against your partner, or your parents, or your kids. Be the rock for your inner child, so that your sense of shame eventually disperses. Build yourself up into a strong enough adult so you can protect your inner child who is hurt and wounded and gets triggered every time someone says your particular trigger word.

Look into the past and admit what happened to you.

Then, think about your traumas and ask yourself these questions:

- What did I learn from that situation?
- It's in the past; it's done – so what am I going to do about it?
- How will I transform this pain into something beautiful in my life?
- Am I going to hang onto these thoughts of victimhood because someone bullied me?

I've been bullied many times in my life. In fact, I survived a period of time when I was a punching bag for various people. One of the lesser bullying experiences happened after I moved to Australia to go to university when I was 20. Because I spoke with an accent and I looked different, I was bullied simply for being Asian. I was picked on by a bunch of juvenile racist kids. And it got to me. It eroded my confidence, making me think I wasn't good

Good Girl

enough, wasn't white enough to live in this country, didn't have equal rights, didn't have the same opportunities and wouldn't go as far as these people. I was a victim then and I felt angry and like I was an outcast. I just wanted to stay home. I'd go to sleep late and then stay in bed until 3 or 4 p.m. the next day, attending classes online and only sometimes going to campus. Although I love make-up, I was wearing too much of it – I'd spend an hour to an hour and a half getting ready to go to class because I was contouring my nose, my cheeks, trying to cover up features I thought were ugly. "I'm not good enough" was the narrative I repeatedly told myself.

I formed my own group of international students, and together we would make fun of the bullies. We'd say mean things about their appearance and the size of their bodies; although I didn't bully them back to their faces, I'd create my own narrative about them. I'm not proud of it and I was young then. This is a minor experience compared to getting your head shoved in a toilet by a bully, which happens to some people, but I'm not invalidating the so-called "minor" incidents of bullying. If you've been bullied, I'm sure it was horrible and it shouldn't have happened to you. I'm deeply sorry, because one way or another, I have experienced all of it – maybe not the same actions, or in the same country or by the same people, but the same emotion. I empathise with you.

They did it and it wasn't fair. You (and I) didn't deserve to be bullied by these people. But it happened, and it's in the past. So, what am I going to do about it? Well, I realised I could write about it, tell people how I survived it, and give people tools to handle it – which is what I'm doing right now.

What are you going to do about your past trauma? You're not there any more, so how can you shape these experiences into something beautiful for yourself? I'm sorry those things happened

Foundation 2: Mental & emotional

to you, but believe it or not, they happened *for* you – because you wouldn't be the person you are today without your experiences. If you were bullied, perhaps you are now more compassionate and would never abuse your power or authority over others because you know what it's like to be on the receiving end. Or maybe you're using your money to bless other people because you were once broke. Our experiences shape our perceptions of the world around us and dictate our actions. When I walk past a homeless person and have money in my pocket, I always give it to them. My friends might say, "Why give it to him, Piyané? That guy's going to use the money for drugs." If he is, that's his karma, not mine; I'd rather give him the benefit of the doubt and assume he's going to buy food. Anyway, what he does with the money isn't my business. Because I know what it's like to not have money to buy food, I don't want to pass up the opportunity to help someone in that situation. You can call me naïve but that doesn't matter. It's my choice. Nobody else's opinion matters any more. I wouldn't be the person I am today without all my experiences – of being poor, depressed, bullied, whatever. Those experiences happened *for* me.

Likewise, you are the kind, compassionate, loving person you are today because you were on the receiving end of the acts of cruelty that you experienced.

Good Girl

My Happy Tunes playlist

Let's end this chapter on a happy note. These are the songs I play on Spotify to perk up my mood. Enjoy!

- *Walking on Sunshine* – Katrina & The Waves
- *Holy* – Justin Bieber, Chance The Rapper
- *Love on Tap* – Beyoncé
- *Put Your Records On* – Corinne Bailey Rae
- *Be the Love* – Adrian Eagle
- *Best Day Of My Life* – American Authors
- *Can't Stop The Feeling* – Justin Timberlake
- *Better When I'm Dancin'* – Meghan Trainor
- *Dancing in the Moonlight* – Toploader
- *Dreams* – Fleetwood Mac
- *Uptown Funk* – Mark Ronson, Bruno Mars
- *All About That Bass* – Meghan Trainor
- *Suddenly I See* – KT Tunstall
- *Sugar, Sugar* – The Archies
- *Lisztomania* – Phoenix
- *Moves Like Jagger* – Maroon 5, Christina Aguilera
- *Everybody Talks* – Neon Trees
- *Move Your Feet* – Junior Senior
- *Ain't No Mountain High Enough* – Marvin Gaye, Tammi Terrell
- *Cake By The Ocean* – DNCE
- *Smile* – Lily Allen
- *Fuck You* – CeeLo Green

Foundation 2: Mental & emotional

- *Girls Just Wanna Have Fun* – Cyndi Lauper
- *I Want You Back* – The Jackson 5
- *All Star* – Smash Mouth
- *Happy* – Pharrell Williams
- *Hey Ya!* – Outkast
- *Here Comes The Sun* – The Beatles
- *Savage Love* – Jawsh 685, Jason Derulo, BTS
- *At My Worst* – Pink Sweat$
- *Dancing in the Moonlight* – Jubël, NEIMY
- *Counting Every Blessing* – Rend Collective
- *Amen* – For King & Country
- *I Want To Break Free* – Queen
- *Rude* – MAGIC!
- *Who Knows* – Marion Black
- *Eulogy* – Ayesha Madon
- *Shake It Off (Taylor's Version)* – Taylor Swift

Foundation 3: Community
(and relationships)

Find the people who have a life you want to live.

"Piyané, I don't have a support network. I don't have people who love me and care about me. I don't have any friends." Is this you?

If so, this Foundation is really important. We all need a community, because self-love only goes so far.

We no longer live in traditional communities, surrounded by friends and relatives who look out for us and automatically help us when we're down. The result is that we might feel lonely and disconnected. Even in a room full of people, we can still feel very much alone. The solution is to build a community of trusted people, person by person.

We all need love, support and connection, and we need it from more than one person. For instance, if you have a spouse, there's only so much that that person can do. Yes, he or she can validate your feelings, but if you keep going back to the same person for the same things, he or she will start to create a narrative about you that may not serve you well. It doesn't mean they are judging you; it just means they are human. They are hardwired to

Foundation 3: Community

calculate and form opinions, whether they want to or not.

Ideally, you have more than one social resource. If your spouse is currently your biggest resource, that's great, but let's expand your social network further than that. We need family and we need friends – good friends we go to for different things. Having just one close friend we go to for everything sounds idyllic but in fact it isn't healthy. Spread the load. You might have one friend who's always up for a trip to the pub: and while that friend is good for drinking a pint of beer with, they're not necessarily the ideal person to confide in about emotionally-laden concerns. Perhaps you have a friend who works at home most of the time, doing the laundry and looking after her kids. She might be someone you can open up to while she is working in the house; but suggest a big night out and she's likely to say she needs to put her children to bed! Or you may be seeking to start a business or you are having problems in your existing business. Perhaps it's not your best bet to look for advice from your best friend who works in a 9-to-5 job, without any idea of what's involved in applying for a Research and Development grant.

Expanding your social circle doesn't mean being disloyal to your existing friends. Yes, some people have one best friend and that's it, but I don't consider this optimal. When you have just one friend for everything, soon enough things will fall apart: a little fight, some jealousy, a bit of "Why are you hanging out with that other person?" Your social circle should be wide enough so that no matter which direction you go, you are assured of support.

For me, finding my tribe didn't happen overnight. Believe me, people weren't knocking on my door and saying, "Piyané, I want to be your friend!" The reality is that if you want something, you must go out and get it. You want a group of girlfriends you can have a slumber party with? Then throw a slumber party, invite a

Good Girl

few people and see who shows up. If no one shows up, now you know that nobody within your current social circle enjoys doing the same things as you. What you need to do is find new friends – and keep doing this throughout your life, as your focus and interests shift.

How do you find new friends? I hear you saying, "I'm in my 30s, I have a 9-to-5 job, I have two kids, a divorce looming, bills to pay. I don't have time to make new friends." Well, you have time on social media, right? That's where you can meet people. Check out friends of friends on social media and send anyone who looks like a potential connection a friend request. If they post a picture of something that interests you, comment on it. Like the photo and comment on it, or send them a DM. Initiate a conversation. Just think, if you can go on dates with strangers from online dating, why not go on "dates" with women you like on social media?

As I said, nobody's going to come knocking on your door; you have to take that first step. Also, if you wait around for people to approach you, you won't have many options. You might be stuck with people who are desperate to find friends and with whom you have nothing in common. Instead of trying to build a friendship with someone who isn't a good fit, target the people who have a life you want to live. Be bold enough to engage with them and don't take it personally if they reject you. Because you will get a lot of rejection: people will leave your messages unread, or read them but not respond to them. It's not personal – after all, they don't know you well enough to not like you. Any loathing you may feel is self-loathing, projected outwards. We don't like rejection because it validates the parts of ourselves we don't like. We believe that not being good enough is why others don't want to hang out with us. You might be afraid that if you get rejected

Foundation 3: Community

by someone it's going to validate those feelings. Be bold. Shrug off the rejections. Keep moving. You will find your tribe.

You need a tribe behind you.

To get anywhere in life, you need a community. I cannot build the things I build without a big team behind me! For all my social platforms, for example, I've had four or five people working behind the scenes. You might be reading this, thinking, "I don't have those kinds of resources, Piyané. I don't have the money to hire people." I hear your frustration. My team isn't just my employees. I have a close friend who is a successful YouTuber who helps me with creatives, and another close friend who's a very good videographer who helps me with filming and equipment – as well as many others to lean on.

Also, know that I didn't wake up one day and have everyone in my life who is there now. I made a decision to change, to attract better things and people, and so can you. If what you're doing isn't working, let's fix it.

Nurturing new relationships and finding your community takes time, so be patient with the process. Right now, I'm still widening my tribe. I feel it's not big enough, because although I give a lot, I also consume a lot from my friends. By the way, you should be comfortable with the notion of taking from your friends. People-pleasers are reluctant by nature to take from anyone, so you must get used to the idea that taking is okay. Remember, you're not just taking selfishly; you're also giving generously.

Authentic relationships begin when we show up as our authentic selves. To be authentic is to be vulnerable. You cannot start an authentic friendship by trying to impress someone ("Look at my new Gucci belt!"). When I suggest you start from a place of vulnerability, I don't mean vomiting all your trauma on them; just

Good Girl

be your comfortable self. If you're someone like me who swears like a trooper, just do it! Be yourself and you will attract people who like you. Authenticity is when you are being truly yourself, and then it's okay to be rejected. If that happens, you might feel hurt but it's important not to stay there. You need to understand that it's not personal: it just means this particular person is not for you and that's fine.

During my life I've said goodbye to many friendships that no longer served me. There are friends who have told me straight up that they can't be friends with me any more because the path I'm on doesn't align with theirs, and I've accepted it on the chin. Sure, I got hurt over it, I lost sleep and cried – because I disagreed with them. I thought we'd merely had a little fight, and my view is that it's overly hasty to throw friends away over one incident. Again, though, I can't control other people. I can only control myself and what I do. And what I can do is widen my social circle and find people who can be there for me, knowing I will be there for them, just as fiercely. Be willing to be your most vulnerable self with people and be willing to reciprocate.

"But I'm giving, Piyané! It's always give, give, give and I receive nothing in return!"

My sweet angel, I hear you. It's incredibly heartbreaking when it's not reciprocated. You've been pouring your energy into a pot with a hole – a bottomless pit. Pour into a different pot. Find a new person. This is not your person. When you give freely and expect nothing in return, who comes back and gives you the same, *that's* your person. Keep giving, but not to the same mother-fucker who never gave anything back to you, okay?! Give to others and make sure you are the biggest blessing to anyone who walks into your life.

Since starting the journey to live my second life, I've wanted

Foundation 3: Community

people to walk into my life and leave in a much better place. I don't always succeed, but that is my intention. Instead of asking, "What can you do for me?", I ask, "What can I do for you?" I'll give recommendations, offer help, give whatever I can see someone needs. If you're struggling to build your own website, I'll pass on the name of someone who did an excellent job for me at a great price. You're stuck in Thailand and need some local contact to help with your passport? I've got you. You need to cry on someone's shoulder at 2am. I'm here. Just give, and in return allow them the opportunity to give to you.

It feels good to give – the act of giving is itself a gift. You are giving to people because it makes you feel wonderful, so give that gift to someone else: it will make them feel good to do something for you. Believe it or not, this is a gift to them. *You* are a gift to them. I might message my friend and say, "Hey, I need help. I'm actually not in a good space. Do you have five minutes to talk to me?" By doing this, I'm gifting my friend the opportunity to be a hero today. When you allow your friend a five- or ten-minute space to listen to your story, they will walk away from that conversation feeling they've done something good today. Just ensure you're not overstepping their boundaries, draining them or being an emotional vampire.

How can you tell if someone is right for you or not? You'll feel it in your gut. As we all have different hobbies and views on life, I can't judge who would be a good fit for you.

Put yourself out there. Get more rejections. The worst thing someone can do is to say no to you. So what? It's no big deal. Move on. And once you have one friend, then you make another and you have two, then three – and now you have the start of a community. Now you can tell a friend about an upsetting moment in your day and they'll lift you up: "Ah, don't worry about

Good Girl

it. I've experienced that too." Friendship is the greatest emotional safety net we can have.

Humans used to live in tribal communities, something now lacking in our era of on-screen communication. Back then, if someone didn't catch food but you did, you'd share with them, and vice versa when you had no food. If someone else was doing well but you weren't, they'd help you improve your situation, and you'd reciprocate. Children were raised by the whole community.

Today the buzz-word is self-love, which is great and I'm all for it, but self-love will only get you so far. The key is love, love for everyone. And it starts with loving yourself and knowing your worth. Know that you are worthy of being in any room with any other people, no matter who they are. You're worthy of being loved and sharing love. It starts with how you're feeling now. So if you're feeling shit, that you don't have anyone you can talk to, that you lack a support network, how are you going to feel worthy of being loved by those people out there? People can feel your energy. If you're giving from a sense of "lack", you most likely won't attract people with abundant mindsets. It all starts with how you feel about yourself. If you want to take on positive energy from others, you have to meet them with the same energy. Better yourself – your mood, your state of mind, your actions – and you will attract people who are the same.

A close friend of mine is a leading hairdresser and make-up artist in Australia. If I say "Can you do my hair and make-up in Singapore? I'm doing a shoot here," she'll respond, "No problem; I'll fly over." You might ask, "Piyané, how do you find all these amazing friends who are willing to do incredible things for you?" Why would she do that favour for me (which she actually did last week)? It's because I'm willing to do the same for her. And if I want to receive her good energy, I need to have a bagful of good

Foundation 3: Community

energy to give back to her.

Soon enough you will outgrow some of the friends you made along the way. You'll probably feel sad letting go of them, and that's fine too. Life is a marathon, not a 100-metre sprint; somewhere along the way you'll be thrown together again and say, "Ah! Hello there! It's been a while. How have you been?"

It's okay to ghost your friends sometimes. With some of my friends, I can go days or even weeks without responding to their messages, and they're okay with that. They know that my love for them is not reflected in how many messages I sent or how quickly I respond to theirs. Not only do they understand that I have a purposeful life to lead, but they respect it.

With some friends I've known for years, we often don't see each other for months, but then we'll catch up for coffee and it's as if no time has passed. Wonderful! I might not have responded to their messages of "How are you? How are things? I'm thinking of you" for a week or two – which possibly isn't ideal – but they know I didn't do that deliberately. If they take it personally, then they don't know me well enough. What I'm communicating is, "Yes, you're my friend, but there are other priorities in my life. I sure hope that I'm not your number one priority in life." That is, unless the message is "Piyané, I need you. Please call me." Then I'll respond immediately.

Some friends will try to tear you down in the name of friendship: "Why aren't you returning my phone calls?" My answer would be, "I've got a life to live! I've got no time to respond to messages right now." Do you have friends who do that? Perhaps they do it in a teasing way: "Yo! I've been trying to reach you. You're not taking my calls?" Your friends are meant to lift you higher and help you do better in life, not drag you down. Friends are there to promote your happiness, to love and support you, and vice versa.

Good Girl

Anything less than that and they're not friends; they're just using you or you're using them because you don't have anyone else. Maybe sometimes you make excuses for them because you don't have other people to turn to.

Years ago, I used to believe I was a burden. I didn't want to call my friends when I wasn't in a good space in case I brought them down. The truth, however, is that high-frequency friends won't be brought down by your energy when you're low. And for you, this is an opportunity to climb up to their energy level. Besides, you'll do the same for them: bring them up to a better emotional place when they are feeling low. The key is to bring each other up to a higher level without draining each other.

It never occurred to me that friendships were supposed to be this way. The message I got from my family growing up was "Don't make friends – they're useless and a waste of time." Looking back, I suspect it's because my parents didn't grow up with a wide enough circle to understand that there are friends who will love them and be there for them and not take anything from them. They were raised in a traditional, oppressive environment in Cambodia (which is, thankfully, no longer the norm). During my upbringing, I struggled to adjust from my parents' Pol Pot era mentality to my own modern era. It was hard having my experiences invalidated – being told by women that I was beautiful and should therefore sew and not go to school, for example. It was a bit like *Bridgerton*: young women were pitted against each other to find a husband, and anyone who was more beautiful and feminine than you was a threat! Therefore, I didn't grow up feeling it was safe to be friends with other women. I didn't know who to trust or who would be a good friend for me, and I'd make excuses for people – "Oh, they behaved badly towards me because I did this or that." Or I would simply isolate myself altogether.

Foundation 3: Community

You need to elevate yourself, and if that means dropping a friend who is constantly operating at a frequency that drains you, that's alright. Or, as I prefer to think about, keep them at arm's length for a time. I prefer not to cut friends and family out of my life completely – I might return to check up on them later on – but I refuse to match people's energies any more. If you hang out in a circle where your friends are always gossiping, the only way for you to bond with them is to produce some juicy titbit about someone else. If you feel you have to match their energy, then you're not aligned. You need to be a rock: solid on your own. Or a crystal which attracts and manifests anything in its gravitational pull. You do not have to lower your energy to match anyone else's. My brain-cells die from conversations I don't feel aligned with – I'm not interested in what a celebrity did last week, for instance. Yet that's how some women bond. If you have to fake an identity to fit in, you won't build authentic relationships.

Be your authentic self, speak your mind, stand your ground. Use your voice and stay firm. In that group of friends who love gossiping, you could say, "We should probably stop talking about this. It's none of our business." And if no one agrees with you, great – now you know that none of these people are your people. If one of them does agree with you, then that person is a potential friend. The way to convert those with friend-potential into real friends is to take the initiative and be true to yourself.

But it can be hard to open yourself up like that. I know, because seven years ago I was miserable and felt ashamed of it, so I hid it by posting pretty pictures on Instagram and Facebook. I'm no longer ashamed of the fact that back then I was thinking about ending my life, because I know I'm not alone. There are plenty of others with similar struggles. So, please know that it's okay to open up and share. Sometimes we don't talk about what we're

Good Girl

going through because we suspect people will gossip about us afterwards. The truth is that while people might gossip about you for a few minutes, they always go back to talking about themselves, because that's their focus. Think about it: when you're on a video call, are you studying and assessing the other participants? No, you're more likely looking at yourself! I do it too! ("Oh my hair looks great today!") So let other people talk if they want to; soon enough they'll be going back to thinking about themselves again. And remember that when people judge you, it reflects something about them that they don't like. It's not about you. Break the taboo about mental health and talk about it.

Confidence is knowing you have value to give to others.
Confidence isn't walking into a room thinking you're better than everyone; that's arrogance. Confidence is walking into a room knowing you're *equal* to everyone. It's knowing that you are as valuable as anyone else in the room, and have just as much to give as them.

I've met many influential people and I've even invited some of them onto my podcasts. I don't want to name-drop, but I do want to say that I'm not intimidated by people with power and influence. I know my purpose. I'm not doing what I do to gather fame or admiration from others.

Walk into a room exuding the energy of "everyone is equal", and you'll be able chat to anybody.

I didn't have many friends in my 20s and early 30s because I believed I wasn't good enough. I lacked confidence and felt I didn't fit in anywhere. But when I started to work on myself and understand my value and what I can bring to people, I understood that my pure existence is a gift. This is not an egotistical statement, by the way: my presence is a gift to you just as much

Foundation 3: Community

as your presence is a gift to me.

You – yes, *you* – are a gift to those around you, including me.

When I walk into a room these days, I never feel like I don't belong. If the conversations are only draining me, I leave because I realise I simply have nothing to offer.

When you walk in not feeling confident, or feeling you don't belong, then you'll be desperate for connection. But when you feel whole, your perspective changes. You think, "I like this person. What can I do for them?" We're here to elevate each other, to lift each other up. And there's plenty of room up here for everybody; we don't need to tear anybody down. If it's not a good fit with someone, walk away. If it is a good fit, think about how to enrich that person's life.

With that mentality in mind, trust me, you attract the right kind of connections and networks. You attract the right type of energy. And even if I choose to leave an event early, not having made any good connections or had particularly valuable conversations, I never feel it was a failure. I'll think, "Oh, well, I dressed up, I looked nice, I got a few photos out of it, and I got some food. I had a good night." That's enough for me.

Nobody is born with skills. Skills come from repetition and practice, and you have to keep flexing those muscles. That includes attending events and mingling with people to hone your social skills and to diminish any associated anxiety.

For me, networking isn't all about work; connecting with others is something I truly enjoy. I like getting to know people and hearing their stories, because they inspire me. You will only live one lifetime if you live with your own story, but if you listen to other people's stories, and you listen with the intention to learn something, you will live multiple lifetimes.

A secret to making authentic connections is to listen without judgement. Be an active listener. That's why we were created with two ears and just one mouth! Remove your ego from the situation, see the wounded inner child in others and extend compassion to them. With every person I meet, instead of thinking, "Oh, that's So-and-So" or "That's a CEO," and seeing them as a title or net worth, I see a human being who will die one day, just like me. This strips away my fear of meeting people. Others often ask me, "How do you even have the guts to talk to that person? How do you walk into a room as confidently as you do?" It's because I throw away people's titles and material possessions and see them for who they are. If they're egotistical, for example, I realise I'm talking to a wounded child.

There are different tactics you can use to speak to different types of people. For instance, if someone just wants to talk about themself, realise there might well be something in that meeting you would benefit from. When I recognise that someone's wounded inner child likes to show off, I can extend my compassionate ears and listen to them. Sometimes beneath the façade, they might say something that surprises me and they might end up having an impact on my life – who knows? A lot of the time, if I take the emotion out of the interaction, I find many people I speak to have things to offer. All I have to do is be a very active listener, and that's a skill you too can develop. It's worth mentioning here that if you have ego issues yourself, you may be blocked by your own ego to the extent that you won't hear what the other person is trying to say.

I wasn't born with the ability to look past people's wounding and listen actively; I developed it over time. I'm not always successful, by the way – sometimes when I'm over-stimulated I can't be a patient or active listener. I would love to improve this skill. Join me and try it next time you're meeting new people.

Foundation 3: Community

Tap into your protector side.

Here's something that will help you in your relationship with yourself and your connections with others. Everyone has both a masculine and feminine side: we each have an inner nurturer and a protector, and it has nothing to do with gender or how we identify ourselves. Men can nurture their children; women can be the boss at work. It's about polarities and complementary energies: yin and yang, sunrise and sunset, active and receptive.

Many women operate from a "feminine" standpoint – sensitive and kind, flowing and receptive – but to solve a problem you need to step into the logical side of your brain. You also need your "masculine" side when it comes to protecting yourself and those you love. For the mothers out there, imagine someone telling you your daughter is ugly. Watch the fire roar! (If anyone so much as comments on my daughter's appearance, I have no problem telling them off.) Or if someone were to attack your mother, your protector side would come out, guaranteed. You'd pull off your heels and earrings and get right in there!

This is the energy I want you to tap into when you notice that you're attacking yourself. Adopt that "fuck off" energy for *yourself*. It's important to be able to draw on your protector energy when necessary instead of acting out on it in an uncontrolled way. For most women, the protector only comes out when we're being pushed into fight-or-flight mode and our defence response is triggered: then we fight. But it's far better to have a clear understanding of your boundaries and the ability to enforce them calmly and firmly, so you don't let situations reach explosion point. If something doesn't sit right with you, you're able to stop it at the source. Instead of agreeing to a request and then breeding resentment because your boundaries have been breached, you say "no" upfront. Some women can go from

Good Girl

"Okay, not a problem" to "Bam!", unleashing the angry protector without warning; it's why we're sometimes called "crazy" and it's a result of not knowing how to access our "masculine" protector side upfront and direct it in a healthy way. Instead of asserting boundaries, many of us let situations we're not comfortable with continue until the situation is completely unacceptable to us, our needs are being trampled, and we're furiously fighting back.

The masculine side is the part of you that conducts business. It's the side that people do not cross, the side that says no, that protects the important people and things and asserts boundaries. You can be extremely sensitive and loving, but the masculine side has to exist, otherwise you will keep pouring out your energy and end up flattened.

Something else to learn is the ability to switch quickly between your masculine and feminine sides. Picture yourself at a networking event: perhaps you're in masculine mode while talking to a very organised man and you're trying to convince him to get involved in your business. Right now you're presenting the ultra-together and efficient side of you: competent, confident, professional, smart. Your logical side is activated. But a minute after your conversation ends, you mingle and grab a coffee and start talking to someone completely different: a beautiful, soulful woman who's a successful actress and singer. Do you think the same mindset will work with her? No, you have to switch to your feminine side. This is not about being fake, if that's concerning you. These are both authentic energies that already reside within you, and you need to draw on them equally in life. Then, when you walk into a room of strangers, you won't feel out of place because you're no longer stuck in one perspective. I can walk into an event and have an hour-long conversation with anyone and enjoy it. This is because I've learned the skill of switching my

Foundation 3: Community

energy. Before, I used to feel I was faking it, acting from "Imposter Syndrome". This isn't to be confused with matching people's energy. When you build enough muscle in both your masculine and feminine sides, you come to see that these are simply communication skills.

Creative people like poets and artists will often tell you they're not good business-people. "Oh, I'm an artist; I'm useless with money," they will claim airily. Why is that? How can someone write you a gorgeous poem or paint you an exquisite picture but be seemingly unable to sell themselves? The truth is that these are skills you have to *learn*. And if you don't learn them, you'll be disempowered in that area of your life. You need to be able to switch from the energy of creating to the energy of logic. Logic requires you to think quickly on your feet: someone's offering you a deal, right now; is it a rip-off or should you pursue it? And equally, if you're stuck in business mode for too long, you won't easily be able to step out of it and do wonderful, creative things. You need to be able to nurture both ways of being – because both are part of who we are.

Though Taylor Swift is younger than me, she's one of my role models. Why? Firstly, she's a boss to the core. She doesn't react rashly; she's in control of her emotions, and this makes her resilient. She can handle criticism because she has two loving parents behind her and a support network to lean on. She doesn't face the world alone.

Secondly, she's a businesswoman *and* a creative, harnessing both masculinity and femininity. Many creatives have loads of femininity and creative flow, but the masculine side is required to run a business, handle the politics and cut through the bullshit, and you need to be able to move adeptly between the two, depending on what the situation requires. Get your head around this mental trick, because it's key to success.

Using your masculine side is a muscle you need to flex. Practise pushing a little bit, often. Be warned: the first time you say no to someone or are assertive with your boundaries, you'll feel like an asshole – like the worst person on earth! And it's okay. Also, sometimes you will make mistakes: "Actually, I'm not the kind of person who accommodates everyone any more, so I'm going to say no," you tell yourself, and then you say no to everything; you overdo the masculine side and actually *do* become an asshole, and that's okay too. Because you're still learning. Allow yourself the space to make mistakes. You're not actually an asshole; you just made a mistake. Don't be quick to attach "I am" to any thought. Remember: if you repeat that too often you will believe it. Stop yourself when you think thoughts that start "I am", and ask, "Is this an 'I am' or an 'I did'?" Are you an asshole or did you just act like one that one time? Learn. Move on. Done.

Keep challenging your thoughts every day. It will be hard, and you might worry that you're losing friends, but personally, I see this as a positive sign. You don't want friends who take advantage of your people-pleasing tendencies. Once you've learned your boundaries and elevated yourself, certain conversations won't sit well with you; perhaps you'll no longer be content to silently witness someone's bullying behaviour just because you love them – you will no longer make excuses for them. You'll stop gossiping about others, because you know it isn't fruitful or good for your mental health. Expect to leave certain people behind. When you keep elevating yourself, at each step you will lose people – but you will also find more.

We all make mistakes, and we will keep doing so. Nobody's a perfect parent, for example. But the worst thing is to acknowledge that we're repeatedly making mistakes yet *keep repeating them*.

Foundation 3: Community

If I'm a people-pleaser and let people walk all over me, I'd be a hypocrite if I told my daughter, "You need to stand up for yourself." If a guy cheats on you three times and you still let him back into your home, what message are you sending to your daughter?

You are the leader in your life. If you have a child, you're the leader of that child. If you have a dog, you're the dog's leader. Even if you live alone, have no friends and no job, you are still the leader of yourself. You are you own soldier, your own general, your own country. Start leading yourself to a better place.

Do a social circle assessment. Now we're going to assess the people in your life in the same way we would a business: by analysing raw data. Get your journal or some paper and answer these questions:

- How many friends would you like to have? Write the answer down. This should be a realistic number, not a far-fetched one.
- Next, how many friends can you count on when you're in need? These are people you can call at 3 a.m. and ugly-cry to.
- Next, how many of your family members do you consider good for your mental health?
- How many people in your life should you be keeping at arm's length? This might include colleagues, your boss, your friends and even your family, who you no longer feel connected to.
- What healthy boundaries do you need to set to protect yourself from people? This will prevent you from reacting to them from a triggered place, which is how you lose people. Next time they invite you to an event, you might make excuses and not go. Write down your reasons: it

- might be because of how they treated you at the last party or wedding you attended with them, for example.
- Who are potential friends in your wider community? Which acquaintances might you want to know better?
- List the people you love who are good for you. Now, for each one, write down the interests and qualities you like in them. Are they kind, compassionate, driven, for instance? Do you appreciate one person's inquiring mind and another person's interest in volunteer work, for example? Which of these qualities do you want for yourself? The qualities you value in your friends will inspire you and help you draw them out in yourself. What are the qualities you have in common with them?
- Now make another list of qualities and interests you would like in your new friends. Be specific. Perhaps you'd like a friend who loves fashion as much as you do. Or music. Or big party nights. (It's fine to go out, have a drink and dance like a silly goose. Have fun but don't be irresponsible, okay?) How will these new friends contribute to your life? Let me assure you, these new people will come. Because it happened for me, I know it can happen for anyone.
- Next, write down how many of each type of friend you would like. For example, "I would like two spiritual friends, who are creative, adventurous, well spoken and well educated."

You might be feeling bad because you think you lack some of those qualities: "Maybe I'm not fashionable enough. Maybe I'm not good enough." If you're feeling unworthy and undeserving of certain friends, you need to explore this. Ask, "What do I need to work on to attract these people?" You're not going to be chasing

Foundation 3: Community

them, acting desperate and trying to convince them to be your friend; you're *attracting* them, and there's a huge difference.

You won't attract someone who's hugely above or below you in frequency or functioning; the difference between you will be small. Say you have on your friendship wishlist a very down-to-earth, happy, contented person who radiates kindness and compassion. Then you need to radiate those qualities too; if not, you'll just be taking from their light. When you're working to be happy and positive, you radiate your own light and will attract the same.

Opposites can also attract when there's common ground. If you love five-star hotels and your friend prefers to "rough it" and camp in the great outdoors, the common ground might be that you simply adore each other's company. You laugh, you tell stories, you fill each other in on the happenings of your life: you care about each other beyond judgement of what anyone wears. What's inside is far more important than the exterior. You love and care for each other and withhold judgement: these are the kind of connections to cultivate.

There are tiers of friendship and you need people in each tier. First is your "go-to at 3 a.m." friend. Your core friend, this might be your best friend, your sister or brother. I know it's a lot of work to maintain a relationship like this, but the reality is that friendships and relationships take work. Then there are friends with specific shared interests, whom you might connect with less often. If you want a wider network, you need to be willing to invest time and energy in it. It is up to you to define what you can give and when you can give it.

Look after your friends, drawing on your protective side when appropriate. Imagine you're with your best friend at a pub and you're both a bit tipsy. You see a guy hitting on your friend, so

Good Girl

you keep an eye on her, and you watch him to see what kind of person he is. And if your girlfriend wants to leave with him, check in with her: "Are you sure you're okay going with him?" Then the most responsible thing to do is to ask her to text you his address. That's what good friends do for each other. They don't just say, "Okay, see ya." No, it's always, "Text me." And you'll send her a reminder: "Where are you? Share your live location with me." Do that for each other so you stay safe.

Whenever you feel insecure about making new friends, hold onto this truth: you are worthy of love from anyone. If someone doesn't give it to you, that is not your problem. Give love to yourself so your cup is full, then look for new friends. When you're a positive, loving person, how likely is it that you will attract a bitchy, manipulative person? You'll have enough self-love, self-respect and intuition to understand that such a person is bad for you – even if you have to learn that by making mistakes. From the fact that you're reading this book, I can assume you've already survived some ordeals in your life. So, trust your intuition and start being honest with yourself.

Now that you've written down how your friends will contribute to your life, answer this last question:

- How can I contribute to them?

Once you are clear on this, you will walk into any room and never feel "less than" because you'll know you have something to give. List your good qualities now: *I am kind, I am a good listener, I am funny, I am intelligent* etc. (Refer to the affirmations in the last chapter if you need inspiration.) With this solid knowledge of what you have to offer, a rejection from someone doesn't seem so personal. You might even think, "Oh well, their loss!" Maybe they're blocking you because it's not the right time. Or maybe

Foundation 3: Community

the universe is protecting you both from something in each other. Who knows? Move on. It's not personal: they don't know you well enough to make a judgement about you so soon. Never jump to the conclusion that you're not good enough to be loved. You might bump into each other later down the line at a party, a work event, a coffee shop, and a friendship might start then. Never leave the door closed: that's my philosophy in life when it comes to widening my circle.

Here's a story about that. If you'd met me when I was 25, you'd think I was the biggest bitch in the world. Not an in-your-face bitch, but more the conniving, jealous type. That arose from my lack of self-esteem, lack of self-love and a whole lot of judgements about myself. If my self-judgements are many, they'll tend to flow from me onto you: judgements about my body, the way I look, you name it. I hated myself back then, so in a room full of people I would stick with those I knew. Had those people who were vibrating on a higher frequency shut the door on me, I would not be where I am today. There's a time and place for everything. There's no need to rush.

Ten years later, I'm a very different person. This goes to show that you never know: someone who's bitchy to you today might embark on a self-development path and become a different person in a few years! Don't label someone based on who they were years ago. Put them aside but keep the door open. Some people change. You're no longer the person you were ten years ago, right? You've grown and developed. That 20-year-old you remember could have evolved into someone far more mature by now. You're not being a fake when you give someone grace; people make mistakes, but I give them the opportunity to prove themselves otherwise, and I don't judge others based on one mistake. Not being quick to judge can only come from a place of

Good Girl

contentment within yourself.

Resentment and anger about people's behaviour will eat away at you. It's like holding fire, so try to let go of it. What people do is about them, not you; it's never personal. You can forgive them but you don't have to let them back into your life. If I'd taken it personally when people who were vibrating at a higher frequency didn't want to befriend me back then, we wouldn't be friends today. Because I'm more confident and comfortable in my own skin these days, I approached one of those people, when we crossed paths recently, and we rekindled a connection. He was big enough to tell me that I'd been bitchy! I remembered how disrespectful I'd been the last time I'd seen him, eight or nine years ago. Here's what happened.

Having spotted him in a coffee shop, I approached him and said hello. We caught up, and I asked him if he'd like to sit down and have a coffee. Sure, he said. We talked about our work, and later he told me, "I've got to say, though, I can't forget the first time we saw each other. I called you 'Pie-yen' and you immediately said, 'My name is Pi-ya-né,' and then you looked me up and down. I'll never forget that! So feisty, girl!" I responded, "Oh, I'm so sorry."

Had he cut me off completely and ignored me in the coffee shop, that would've been him vibrating on a lower frequency, but he's vibrating higher up. And he knew my bitchiness back then was not personal; that's why he was confident enough to bring it up with me. Today I know that his mispronouncing my name when we first met was not a personal attack. How the hell would a stranger know how to pronounce my name? But years ago I had a chip on my shoulder about being in a minority: *Why don't you just ask me instead of butchering my name?* Entitlement oozed out of me, because I was compensating for something –

Foundation 3: Community

for the fact that I was insecure and didn't feel good in my skin. I was looking to feel better about myself by putting other people down.

There are two ways to win in life. Say you've built the tallest building in your city; it has 180 floors. Then, damn! Someone goes and builds a 181-floor building and yours is no longer the tallest. You can blow that building up and remain the tallest building, or you can build another one, with 182 floors. The choice is yours. In that moment of meeting someone who mispronounced my name, I was feeling "less than", so in order to feel superior I put that person down. I chose to bomb the building instead of building a new one, which would have entailed elevating my state.

Even if someone is really bitchy to you, it's not personal, although it might feel that way. It is simply a reflection of them. Someone who is emotionally regulated and content within themselves will never tear you down; they will politely correct you or give you constructive criticism. And, in a work context, someone who's a good leader will show you how to perform a task instead of bossing you around.

My advice is never to cut people off. It was only when I was 30 that I unlearned the belief about friends I'd inherited from my parents. It was hard to act on a new belief at that age, one that went against the grain of what I'd grown up with. My family's assertion, "Friends are useless. Study hard, work hard and prioritise your family", was proven true when I made some friends through trauma-bonding, not genuine love for each other, and we were too insecure and jealous to leave each other or find new friends.

The truth, though, is that some families are extremely toxic and not worth your time. I'm not suggesting you cut your family off, but don't go to them seeking wisdom they can't offer. In general,

Good Girl

don't take advice from people who don't have what you want. You wouldn't ask a homeless person for financial advice. Similarly, you probably wouldn't ask a divorced person for marriage advice. It's not mean to think, "I can't go to Carol for marriage advice because she's divorced"; you're not putting Carol down. You can hang out as friends or go to her for emotional support, and in return you can offer support through her journey through divorce. You can hang out as friends. But if she's saying you should leave your husband, or stay in your abusive relationship, it's probably better to talk your issue over with a marriage counsellor than with Carol. Ask for advice from people who have what you want or from a professional. For many of us, our parents are our go-to people for advice on everything. But if your parents are broke, don't ask for their financial advice, and if they sound judgmental towards each other, don't ask them for relationship advice. Widen your circle to include friends of every type you would like.

Today, I prioritise my family in different ways and I love them very much. I'm there to love and care for them; we have funny conversations and tell jokes, we make fun of each other and hold family gatherings – but I do not go to them for advice I know they cannot give, and then blame them for not being able to give it. That's setting them up for failure and that's not fair.

Making new contacts and friends isn't that hard. It's so easy to stay loosely connected to people today: you don't have to write letters or dial phone numbers; you just check in on social media or messages.

As we end this chapter, I dare you to reach out to someone you haven't talked to for years. Maybe they've changed. (Or maybe they haven't.) They might even start with an apology. If they are still who they were and you don't like it, put them aside again! That's fine too. Yes, you make yourself vulnerable by putting yourself out there, but I dare you to do it. As I've said, people don't come knocking on your door to be friends, and if they do, that's creepy – close the door! They're probably in marketing or insurance sales. (I'm joking... kind of!) Ultimately, if you want to make friends, you have to be brave. Being courageous is not easy, by the way; it's about recognising your fear and going ahead despite it, and feeling that whatever the outcome might be, you can live with it. What's the worst thing that person you're approaching could do? Say no? You might be humiliated a little, but you won't die from that. Great!

TIPS AND TOOLS

- **Practise active listening.**
- **Do your daily Community Foundation work.** This could be texting "I love you" to someone important in your life, or picking up the phone to call someone you love – your parents, your sister, a best friend, a long-lost close friend.
- **Change your relationships in 28 days.** Each day for four weeks, take a small action to improve your relationships: for instance, text someone different every day to say something nice about them and offer them comfort. Developing close relationships gives you a glow of gratitude, and this will motivate you to do more of it. Your social circle will be in much better shape after those four weeks.
- **Thank yourself and the people in your life**. Sit comfortably, close your eyes and calm your breathing. With your head dipped and your hands crossed over your chest, take a deep breath, then thank yourself for everything you do.

Honour yourself. Say, "I thank myself for everything I have done today." And, "I thank the people in my life for being here. Thank you for being here for me today, so I feel connected and not alone."

- **Write a daily contribution list: "Three Things I Did Today that Make a Difference".** This exercise doesn't just work for your personal life; I've been doing this for a while now and it really helps my professional self-esteem. At the end of the day, I write down three to five things of massive value I've given to my team and the people I work with. How did I support them today? What did I do today that quantified my wealth and my companies? Sometimes I look at my list and think, "Wow, look what I did today!" This reassures me that I have valuable, helpful knowledge to pass onto others. You can write this list in your gratitude journal too.

Foundation 4: Spiritual

You need faith in something bigger than yourself.

Let me begin this chapter with a disclaimer. When I say "spiritual", I don't mean religious. I understand that you might be an atheist and find the whole subject of spirituality triggering. In that case, don't use the word "God"; use "source", "universe" or whatever word sits best with you. And if your god comes in the form of a bearded guy or a woman clad in a sarong, that's fine – as long as you're comfortable.

Please also understand that I'm not out to disrespect any religion. In the course of my 37 years I have experimented with many religions. I was born Buddhist and went to the pagoda; I've prayed with my Muslim friends and been to church with my Christian friends; I've explored Hare Krishna and chanted to the sacred little blue boy – and I'm still figuring all this out. I have no hatred or particular leanings when it comes to religion, but if a religious group is trying to convert me to something that goes against my beliefs, I will stop practising it.

What has changed is that I have found my spiritual source: I feel awakened by the fact that the journey of life ends with death. This may sound grim, but hear me out. Everything in the world

Good Girl

has its opposite: night and day, darkness and light, yin and yang. Death's opposite is life, and life's opposite is death. For a long time death was a taboo topic for me, something no one talked about. But I want to talk about it, because your perspective changes when you see your life as a gift – a gift made all the more precious because of the fact that it will end one day.

Let's look at just how remarkable your existence is. From a million sperm, you were the unique being who happened to be created from the single life-force that made it happen. You were the chosen one, and you are here for a reason. Billions of lives have been created by this force and, like all the others, you will go on a journey, and as you progress through life you will accumulate experiences and memories, both good and bad from your perspective.

What will take you to a new spiritual level is the human ability to make something "good" out of something "bad". When you turn a traumatic event into something beautiful, you transform yourself spiritually and find your purpose.

I experienced domestic violence when I was younger. Had I become stuck in victim mode, I would still be living an internal war, continually thinking, "This shouldn't have happened to me. I'm so angry!" But along the way my anger was forged into passion. Now I stand up against domestic violence because I know what it's like to be on the receiving end of a fist or a belt. Yes, that burning passion turned me into a bitch when I was 25, and that's okay; it was part of my development. But now I've matured and discovered a more useful way of thinking.

Basically, there are three perspectives you can take in a situation. The first is yours. To use me as an example, it would be, "Why did my father hit me? I didn't deserve that." The second perspective is the other person's; in this example, my father's:

Foundation 4: Spiritual

"What she did warranted discipline. I love her and want her to learn. This is the only way I know to make my daughter better." The third perspective, which comes from the Source, explains why the situation happened in the first place: "This happened for your ultimate benefit." If my experience hadn't happened, I wouldn't be the person I am today, so this situation happened for the better. Believe it or not, your situation happened *for* you, not just *to* you.

There's always a third perspective in a situation, and the challenge in finding it is overcoming your resentment and victimhood. This is not to invalidate your experiences and hardships, by the way. Those horrid things did happen to you, but that's all the more reason to find a third perspective – and it can only come from faith, faith that your experiences happened to you for a reason – otherwise you will forever be mired in victimhood.

Before I tell you this next story about my parents, I need to point out a few things. I have wrestled with whether or not to include this story in the book. I tell this story not to shame anyone, but to demonstrate the effects of voicelessness and to give an example of turning scars into art. My wish is that you also may begin to think about your own painful and traumatic experiences, to break through your voicelessness, recognising that this may be a starting point for becoming more fully yourself and turning your powerlessness into empowerment.

I also need to point out that I love my parents and we have a really good relationship now. They have grown as people over the years – as have I – and are no longer who they were when I was growing up. So please read it with the same level of compassion for my parents that I have.

These events happened a long time ago and I have forgiven

Good Girl

my parents completely. I'm no longer hurt; something that helped me process it was speaking to therapists and spending time in personal reflection.

I also understand their traumatic history as survivors of the Khmer Rouge, including the murder of many of their closest family members. These horrific experiences fuelled their actions towards me, even if they themselves were limited in understanding how.

So as you read this story, please remember that I'm not telling it from a victim standpoint but simply to supply context, so that you understand how my experiences have made me who and what I am today. Everyone has stories that shape their entire life, knowingly or not. This is one of mine.

Growing up in a conservative family, I often witnessed my parents fighting and saw my father discipline my sister by hitting her. He'd discipline me too, but never to the extent that he did when I turned fifteen.

Picture this. It is December 2001 and have just turned fifteen, and am about to go to High School. I have a good circle of friends and I meet a cute boy. We've been "dating" for a few weeks. By dating, I just mean we often hang out at the cafeteria together and it's really innocent – we've "kissed" once, just a soft peck on the lips under a tree at school, nothing more. He has a motorbike and one day after school he asks to take me for a ride around town before dropping me off at home like he usually does (he drops me a block from my house so my parents won't find out). It's really common in Cambodia to ride motorbikes everywhere, including to and from school. To get from A to B you need your own motorbike or a motorbike taxi, and higher class people will have cars. There are no school buses, public transportation or highways.

I don't have my own motorbike; I get dropped off to school by

Foundation 4: Spiritual

my family and often walked home after school, before I met him, only about fifteen minutes away.

One day the boy asks if we can go for a ride to the riverbank (fifteen minutes motorbike ride away) before he drops me home. I am very excited because it's the first time we venture out of "my" area together. It's so much fun riding on the back of his bike, seeing the river and the people going about their lives – and here I am on the back of a motorcycle with a very cute boy who is so nice to me. Most of the ride is slow and silent, one of my arms wrapped around his waist holding onto him, while one of his hands is on mine protectively, tenderly. We hardly ever touch, so this fills me with butterflies and excitement. I am happy and free for once in my life.

My bubble is soon burst when I see someone I know on the street, a colleague of a close relative. When we catch sight of each other, my face goes white and cold with fear. I know word will get back to my parents that I was on the back of a boy's motorbike, and my parents won't like that, especially my father.

That is exactly what happens; my parents hear about it the next day. Perhaps because of the look on my face when I am seen on the motorbike, my parents are told that I looked "glazed over, as if on drugs". My parents confront me and accuse me of using drugs, and riding on a motorbike with a boy who's influencing me to take drugs. I am shocked. How could they even come up with this? On top of that, they accuse me of having sex with him. *None* of that is even close to being true!

My parents lock me in their room until I confess so they can find a suitable course of action. Each day I am confined to their room while they go to work. I can't leave this room for anything, even for school. I am not even allowed to open the bedroom door.

As soon as my father gets home each day, the interrogations

Good Girl

begin again, followed by increasing physical "punishment" when I keep denying what they accuse me of. At first it is just slapping, but as my denials continue, the "punishment" escalates. The interrogations are the only form of communication – no one talks to me all day other than this, and *that's* how I know I'm in deep, deep trouble.

Within a few days, I've completely shut down, physically and emotionally. I am in shock and terror. I've been beaten in the past just for getting bad grades; so what on earth is my father going to do to me now?

Being so shut down, I don't even say "thank you" when I'm given food; I choose not to talk at all. I am voiceless anyway, so why would I bother? My body might still be here but my mind is far away; if I'm not here, then I can't be hurt.[28]

My parents see my "glazed" state as evidence that I am in drug withdrawal. I have never even heard there's such thing as drug withdrawal. My hands shake from anxiety and fear – but they see this as a further sign of me coming off drugs.

Each day after my father gets home from work, he comes into the room and questions me. Am I using drugs? Am I sleeping with this boy? His questions are always the same but the techniques to elicit a confession are different and unpredictable – on some days he starts slowly and is nice to me: "It's okay, daughter, you can tell me the truth and I won't hurt you. You can trust me." On other days he shouts, swears and hits me.

Days turn into weeks. I'm told I won't be going to school anymore and to forget about seeing my friends ever again. Just like that, my life is over!

---

28 After years of therapy I came to recognise this as my first full-blown experience of dissociation, a common survival technique for people experiencing severe trauma.

Foundation 4: Spiritual

Because I have nothing to confess, this goes on and on, for more than 40 days. No school, nothing but jail in their bedroom. Sometimes my mother is present with my father, also chiming in with the interrogation. At least when my mother is there, I know that the beatings won't be as bad as when it's just my father and me.

Then one day, when my mother is not there, my father does something different. He grabs me by the hair, pushes me to the floor and kicks me when I refuse to confess that I use drugs. I can physically feel his rage and I know he's not doing this just to discipline me; he's unleashing his anger. And I haven't done anything wrong: I'm *not* using drugs; I *haven't* slept with the boy!

But I know I deserve some discipline because what I did was not "good". I'm supposed to be a "good girl", not touching anyone or even being seen with a guy until I'm married. I was just on the back of a boy's motorcycle. Surely I don't deserve this? Surely this isn't right?

My father continues and eventually everything blacks out. Later, when I come to, I look up and see my father towering over me. I try to turn my head but I can't – he is standing on my neck! I can't breathe and I can taste bile in the back of my throat. My father moves his foot to kick me again and again in the stomach, and I scream for my mother, "Mak." Most of the screams come out as whimpers: "Help, Mak! Mak!"

And no-one comes to help.

This all happens in a blur. I don't remember much, but I do remember this: I. Am. Going. To. Die.

I do the only thing I know I can do to get out of this. I lie. I tell my father, "Yes, I *did* use drugs."

He shouts back, "What drugs?"

I say the first thing I can think of. I don't even know what heroin

Good Girl

is, but I remember it from the news on TV.

"Heroin," I reply. "Please stop, please don't kill me."

* * *

The nightmare was not over. In the days to follow, my parents worked to elicit all the gory details of my "drug usage" from me; when and how it began, what I used... to be honest, I don't remember much of what I said. I mentally checked out. That is the essence of "dissociation". It was like someone else was there in my place, concocting a story to convince them that I was telling the truth, to rescue me from punishment.

I didn't even flinch as the vile lying words came out of my mouth. I knew I was safe in a far away corner, tucked away in my brain, while another part took over and protected me with all the lies my parents wanted to hear.

That day broke me. My physical body, my heart, my soul, my spirit, my dignity were all stripped away – everything that made me human, as I watched myself from a corner of my brain telling them all these stories like a robot. That was the day I lost all hope in humanity. That was the day I learned the truth, staying true to myself and maintaining dignity is bullshit. It's not safe. My father had hurt me to such a degree that I'd had to betray myself. When I had no other choice but to admit to things I hadn't even done, I learned that I was not even safe in my own body. I learned that I had to very carefully guard what I said as a matter of life and death.

This deeply shaped my whole belief system about my worth and how I then navigated life for many years to follow. From then on, it was all about survival. I developed significant trust issues. I questioned all sorts of authority. The world I had known was no longer safe. I couldn't trust anyone, so I was all alone. I knew I was

Foundation 4: Spiritual

not – and never would be – good enough. I remember singing in the room absently, it was a sad love song. My sister quickly came in to tell me to hush or they would hear it and assume I was longing for my "boyfriend". So I stopped singing. In fact, I stopped singing for a very long time. The trusting, playful, artistic, singing Piyané who existed before all this, was now a shadow tucked away in a corner in my mind. She was what I later came to know through therapy as the "abandoned inner child" or, in spiritual language, the "shadow self".

I later found out my friends came to find me multiple times because by this point I had disappeared from school for almost six weeks. My parents told them and everyone who questioned my absence, including the neighbours, that I have gone to study in Thailand. The boy in question also came looking for me multiple times – he knew the truth because I told him that day that I would be in deep trouble for having been seen with him. He was relentless. He was in High School, two years older than me. When my parents shooed him away multiple times, he came back with his uncle and father and even asked for my hand in marriage in an attempt to rescue me from it all. This was probably the most romantic thing anyone had ever done for me to that point. Of course my parents refused, replying that I was only fifteen and he was seventeen, and they courteously told them to come back when I was eighteen. The boy was persistent and threatened to report them to the police because they shouldn't be able to imprison me like this. Maybe now that there were other adults involved, or maybe because they found my confession convincing – or for what other reasons I still don't know, my parents let me go back to a different schedule of school soon after that, so that I wouldn't see my friends or the boy anymore.

By then I had spent nearly two months in house arrest. I was

Good Girl

dropped off and picked up from school by my mother. Everything I possessed including clothes, school notes and backpacks, were all regularly ransacked. I went to school everyday and didn't make friends because I was forbidden to.

This all went on for a few more months until my parents announced one day that they would move to the US and leave us behind for a few years until they could get us there also. It was (selfishly) the happiest day of my life. At the airport, my father hugged me and told me that everything they do, they do for me. I scoffed on the inside but kept a straight face, hugged them and told them to travel safely.

He then said something I would never forget: "Don't be too eager for your parents to be gone. You will soon find that the world is very cold without your parents protecting you." I didn't understand it at the time; I just couldn't wait for them to leave so I could be free. I soon discovered that the world was indeed actually very cold, but those stories are for another time.

I locked that memory away for over a decade. I didn't want to go there, didn't want to touch it. I didn't think much of it in my 20s, even though those experiences had secretly driven my life. Despite not thinking of it actively, a driving factor for me was the belief – even the knowledge – that I was not "worthy". And when I started going to therapy at the age of 30, in recovery from my depression and suicidal ideation, I happened to mention it to my therapist in passing, very casually. My therapist was in shock, and there began the process of unpacking my old trauma.

It's amazing what your mind will do to protect you. I have learned from therapy and wide reading in this area, that suicidal thoughts are not there to punish you; rather, they are your brain's own kindness, its attempt to give you a way out. Your brain is a computer and when you're in terrible pain, suicide is sometimes

Foundation 4: Spiritual

the only escape it can imagine. You might walk along a cliff path, look down, and think, "Hmm, what would happen if I jumped...?" It's only an intrusive thought, and you have the agency to believe which thoughts you should act on and which ones you shouldn't. A sensible response would be not to jump. But when you're depressed and anxious and you have lost your sense of self and worth, you don't know *which* thoughts to believe in any more.

That is when you're in trouble: when you don't know who you are or what you're worth. Whilst tragedy can happen in the blink of eye, it can bring about many very painful emotions. However, depression, anxiety and suicidal ideation don't just arise overnight. We don't wake up one day and suddenly become depressed or suicidal. These conditions are not just the result of one mistake that we have done or one mistake that others have done to us. They take days, weeks, months, years or even decades to build up, and are often the result of trauma or abuse, whether self-inflicted or from others. That is when we need help.

As I've said, this traumatic story of mine happened many years ago and I'm done seeing myself as the victim, although I did so for a very long time. I'm not discounting what happened to me. But I can now see that what happened *to* me, happened *for* me.

We often hear there are two sides to every story, but there are actually three.

Three sides to every story:
A tree cannot grow to touch heaven, unless its roots touch hell.

The first side
The first side in this story is mine – I was the victim and had to betray myself, to lie – in order to survive. This had great

Good Girl

consequences for me for many years.

The second side
The second side is my parents' side. My father loved his little girl and wanted to protect her in the only way he knew how. He went through his own very traumatic upbringing through the Khmer Rouge regime, where his family was slaughtered. To this day, I still don't know the details of what happened because he has told me very little about it. My mother was just eleven when the Khmer Rouge began, and seven members of her family of eleven, including both her parents and five siblings, were murdered in the regime.

The Khmer Rouge regime used severe measures such as family separation, starvation, torture, medical experiments and outright murder, to keep people in line. Therefore, from the earliest age, both my parents had learned violence as the way to discipline.

I have full sympathy for what they have survived and I admire their grit and perseverance to rise above all of this, to bring up both myself and my sister in a loving home.

This story is just one story, one mistake they made. I could also tell a million other stories of their success in loving me and keeping me safe as their daughter. Though we didn't have much in terms of material resources, my parents looked after me very well and did their best with what they had; they were teaching me at the level at which they had been taught. I was and am blessed to be their daughter.

While living under their roof, I never once went to bed hungry, or feeling hot or cold. Not even an insect bite went unattended. There was never an occasion when I was sick under their care, without either or both of them by my side, day and night. I know in my heart they both love and cherish me very much – I know my parents are beautiful people. Yes, they've made mistakes – and

Foundation 4: Spiritual

so have I.

The third side
The third side to this story is from what I call the "Source". If you are religious, you might call this "God". Or there might be other words you can relate to. It's like the air we breathe, the gravity we feel. You can't see it, but it's there; whether you want to acknowledge it or not – it's there.

For me, if all of that happened, *just* to happen, then what's the point? I'd be a victim forever. Even after understanding my parents' side of the story, this didn't necessarily help me fully heal. While I can understand their actions, I can't understand why it's happened to me.

So I asked the Source, my higher self, *what is this experience trying to teach me?* What can I learn from this? The answer is very simple.

If this event hadn't happened, I would not know what it is like to be voiceless and powerless. I would not understand what it feels like to have all my rights stripped away. Had I not been on the receiving end of all this, I would not know how to use my voice or power for the good of others. I wouldn't know that kindness, understanding and patience are desperately needed in this world.

In saying this, I'm not claiming to have mastered all of these virtues. But I do know this: I will never knowingly abuse my power. This experience was a gift to me.

The Source has guided me towards my purpose – my mission. However, whilst I have promised to be authentic in telling you the truth, I will keep my own mission in life to myself. This part is sacred. It's between me and the Source. One thing I can tell you however: A tree cannot grow to touch heaven, unless its roots touch hell.

Good Girl

The universe aligns to make things happen for you

Faith is not religion, unless you want it to be. If there's someone you pray to, imagine that they made your experiences happen for a reason, for you. Or, if you lack faith in any religion or deity or person, have faith in those who came before you. Faith is bigger than us; it is about collective information and collective experience. It's not something that you own; it is something you get to experience. You know the hope you hold onto when you're feeling very low, that little voice in your head telling you there's something out there for you? That's faith.

"But Piyané, I don't have faith. How do I get it?"

We'll start small, by looking for the little miracles that happen in your life. This will show you how the universe aligns to make things happen for you. Then we'll talk about manifestation, because once you have faith you'll believe in manifestation.

If you don't have faith, you can borrow mine. Believe that you are worthy of love beyond measure and all the good things you wish for. The universe has made you who you are, the way you are, on purpose; it's no coincidence. And you deserve love. Feeling this can only come from faith. You might say you don't have faith, or perhaps religion and spirituality are triggering topics for you and you don't want to venture into woo-woo land. That's not a problem. Just take my faith – because you won't go far without it. Without faith in something bigger than yourself, life will be rough. I guarantee you will stop on the journey upward if you don't cultivate faith, because you will be detached from the Source and from collective information. I was an atheist once. I didn't believe in anything; it was all *me, me, me* – and it felt so lonely.

Without faith, you will only be serving yourself. People-pleasing is not about pleasing other people; you're actually doing it to

Foundation 4: Spiritual

please yourself – to satisfy your need to feel good enough and important and wanted and a nice person, someone who doesn't fight or cause problems. You'd be lying to yourself and to me if you told me, "I'm just a very agreeable person." No, you're not. You have your own opinions when someone is being an asshole, don't you? Or when someone crosses you? You don't necessarily say it out loud, but you think those thoughts. When someone does something to you that you intuitively know is wrong, your people-pleasing tendencies might overrule your instinctive behaviour, which is to stand up for yourself, draw boundaries and communicate clearly. This is your birthright, but you refuse it because you're pleasing yourself. Sure, you might be pleasing other people but you're also pleasing yourself, because you want to be liked and to feel important. You want to be loved, but you end up betraying yourself in the process. It's still all about *self*, without a collective purpose. Continue this way and you will lose yourself altogether.

Your purpose has to be much bigger than you. Say your plan is to make a million dollars in two years. That amount will satisfy you for a while – you'll spend some of it, splurge on your family – but what then? Next, you're going to need another two million dollars because you can't keep having the same experiences, right? You'll want bigger, better things. And once you're in the million zone you'll start making friends who are millionaires, and because they have better, nicer things than you, you'll have to spend more and more to feel like you measure up.

Gratitude starts where greed ends. Having gratitude for the things you possess is a total game-changer. Everything you have in your life now, was what you once wished for.

We've all experienced this: we might think about someone and then suddenly they send us a message or call us, or we

Good Girl

unexpectedly bump into them. And there have been times when we've needed help and assistance appeared, seemingly out of nowhere. We have thought, "Wow, that's such good luck!" It's not luck; it's the universe conspiring to make our life easier, to help us manifest the things we want.

Now that we're on the topic of manifestation, I'm going to venture into territory you might dislike. All the bad things that happened to you? You manifested them too. You manifested your bad relationships, your stressful financial situation, your mean boss. These were manifested from your subconscious because deep down you felt unworthy. If you don't feel worthy of a good relationship, for instance, you will keep manifesting a bad one.

Take my faith and believe that there is someone or something out there who loves you unconditionally and is working in your favour. That's why you are here. You're still here, right? You have two eyes that are reading my book, or maybe you are listening to the audiobook with your two ears. These are things that some people can only dream of. Plus, you have a roof over your head, water you can drink – so much that you can be grateful for.

Believe that the things that happened in your life are given to you as gifts. Once you start looking at everything in your life as a gift and not as an entitlement, you will be transformed. By the way, nothing in your life is permanently yours. In 50 years' time someone is going to live in that house you're working so hard for now. In a while, someone else is going to be driving your car – and maybe it'll be some drunk teenager! The job you're so proud of will one day be obsolete. Nothing in life is permanent; everything is borrowed. Even your life is borrowed; like everyone else, you will meet the end one day. So, take my faith and believe that something out there is conspiring to work in your favour. Then you'll start seeing that the things that happen in your life

Foundation 4: Spiritual

are gifts. If not, you'll have an attitude of entitlement: "I worked hard for this house, Piyané! What do you mean? I *earned* this. This is *my* house!" Yes, for the time being, it is, but that house isn't going to be yours forever. When you're gone, who will it belong to? "My child!" you say. Well, she's not going to live forever either. And maybe she'll want to sell the house and go backpacking around the world.

Once you see that everything is borrowed, that everything is a gift, you will live from a place of abundance. You'll think to yourself, "I'm so grateful for everything I have in my life: for working hands that can flip these pages and hold this glass of water so I can drink it. I'm so grateful I have legs that can carry me from A to B..."

Gratitude and contentment are entirely different from toxic positivity and chasing the fleeting emotion of happiness. Perhaps the thought of too much contentment unsettles you: if you're happy with everything as it is, how will you still have vision and motivation to improve yourself? Don't worry – when you have faith, a sense of purpose naturally follows. When you start to receive abundance, you will instinctively want to give, and then you'll be inspired to work from a higher frequency. There will be purpose attached to the dollars you're making. Now you're not just working for yourself; you have a higher purpose and it's not just *self, self, self* any more. Perhaps you'll want to build orphanages, or travel the world so you can learn more and share more.

People with faith vibrate at a different frequency and they give on a different level. Others might say, "Wow, you're so kind! Why would you do that for me?" When you have faith, you believe life is a gift and you want to share your happiness and gifts with others. Simple.

Good Girl

I'm made for a bigger reason.

Let's go back again, to 2018. I'm alone in my bedroom at 2 a.m., crying hysterically and banging my fists on my mattress. I'm not crying about anything specific but I'm in so much emotional pain that it feels unbearable. *Why do I even exist? Why is all this happening to me? Why am I feeling this way? There's no way out for me! I just want the pain to stop! My mother always told me how my life should be and I'm living it! Everyone says I'm lucky and should be feeling blessed, so why am I not happy? Why do I want to jump off this building? I must be stupid!*

It's the middle of the night and I've had my bath drawn for hours. An idea comes to me: before I take my bath I could take a handful of Valium – that would be the perfect way out. But before I do that, I'm just going to do something else. I'm going to have a big argument with this so-called God that everyone prays to. So I start petitioning God. I shout out, "If you are real, God, FUCK YOU! If you created me, why are you doing this to me? Why is this happening to me? Fuck this, God! What plan do you have for me?" I'm banging on the mattress in frustration, anger, sadness, every emotion under the sun, on and on and on.

I don't remember how long this went on for, but at some point I happen to look out the bedroom window at the city lights. From my particular angle as I hit the mattress, I see something strange outside. The streetlights have formed letters, and I pause to read them. I see a P... I... Y... A... N... and... is that an E? Oh my god, no way! *The streetlights have formed my name from this angle!*

Then silence. I've been crying so much that I don't even hear my own voice any more. And now that I've stopped crying, the silence is huge.

I stare at my name made in lights down there in the city streets and I say, "Okay. okay." And then comes this thought: *I'm made*

Foundation 4: Spiritual

for a bigger reason.

I haven't told many people this story until now because it sounds a bit crazy. People will tell me, "You'll see what you want to see, Piyané." They're right; I saw what I wanted to see that night – because underneath it all, I didn't want to die. I just wanted the pain to stop. And seeing my name in the streetlights was the first sign, because if you want the pain to stop, you need faith. You need faith in yourself; you need to believe that you can do it. And I said, "Okay. I can do it."

Recalling that night still makes me emotional, seven years later. God – or the universe, or whatever you call it – didn't call my bluff because I wasn't bluffing. I was for real. That night was the first time I had a genuine conversation with God. (And as you can tell, it wasn't a pleasant and polite conversation. It wasn't, "Dear Lord..."; it was full of the F-word and pure anger.) The fact that some force was so loving towards me in that moment, when I really needed it, moves me hugely. I just needed a sign right then *and I reccived it.* That was the moment I understood I was made for a greater purpose. If this could happen to someone who felt as low as I did, who felt so useless that killing herself seemed the only thing worthy of her – if a force so powerful could arrange things so I could see the lights that would save my life – then I had to have faith.

This is an extremely deep and personal story to me. This experience, in my darkest moment, changed me from being a complete atheist to believing in God. And when I say "God", I don't mean any figure in particular; I mean the universe, a creator, a force that's bigger than me. I'm now someone who knows there is a huge, loving force out there that supports my best interests. I still have a lot a work to do on my faith, but that was the pivotal point in my life: *Piyané, every single time you feel like you're not*

Good Girl

worthy to live, know that you are. Since that moment, I've never believed I'm not worthy of living. If the thought does pop up, which it does regularly, it gets snapped away quickly because the light is brighter. And I want to spread that light with you. If anyone out there is open to it, they will receive this message.

The streetlights forming my name are still there. A couple of new high-rise buildings are blocking part of it – Melbourne has grown and developed – but the name is still visible from my apartment window.

How did I get from there to where I am now? The truth is that I've worked hard, internally and externally, to reach the place I'm in today. After that extraordinary night, I thought, "Where do I even begin?" Then I asked myself, "What needs to stay in my life, and what needs to go? Let's start with people. Who needs to go? Who needs to stay?" A bunch of people popped up in my mind: *These are the ones who have your back, P. You need to trust your instincts. Say tomorrow a whole new "you" wakes up. Who do you want in your life? You get to pick and choose, right now. You choose who goes and who stays. You also choose where you live...* Suddenly, I thought, "Oh wow, I'm free! I get to choose! I have options!"

My old identity started to fall away. This was the first step to being free from my depression: the fading away of the old me, the one who was saddled with all the expectations and standards of being a "good girl". I'd grown up with very strong messaging: "You should be doing this, Piyané, you should be saying this, you should be dressing like this, behaving like this." All that noise just started receding: the expectation to be married by a certain age, to have kids at a certain age. Anyway, I'd done all those things by the book: I met my partner when I was 20, got married at 25, had a baby at 28. By the time I was 30 we were multi-millionaires;

Foundation 4: Spiritual

we had homes and businesses, and we travelled the world. On paper it was all perfect. This is the definition of every girl's dream, right? Have children, have a career, have a nice home and live a good life – what else do you want?

But all those achievements hadn't given me a good life; in fact, they had just made me really, really depressed, because I was *living someone else's identity*. It was someone else's dream and I hadn't had the time to discover who I was or what I wanted. At age 30, I didn't understand that I needed to heal from my past, to grow and blossom. At the time, I didn't understand where my depression and anxiety came from. Now I know it was because I was feeling confined by an identity that wasn't mine to begin with, and I needed to start living my own dream. But since I had never been encouraged to pursue my identity or dreams, I didn't even know where to begin.

The problem with making big changes is that most of us are scared of our own minds. We fear our shadow sides. It's why the entertainment industry and social media and distraction industries in general are so successful: keep scrolling and you'll keep distracting yourself from those dark thoughts. Yet once you've faced your fear, nothing else will matter. Don't go there alone, though. Go there with faith – and take my faith if you lack your own. Just believe that someone out there is conspiring to make your life better.

To bolster your faith, consider your power of intuition – where does it come from? Why do some of us prefer chocolate ice cream and others prefer vanilla? We think we choose this preference, but do we? It's in your genes, yes, and who put it there? The thousands of ancestors who came before you and whose genetic material constitutes your own put it there. If you're averse to the word "God" or any of my other suggestions, use "ancestors", because that long line of people who came before you is undeniably real.

Born in a country with a recent history of trauma, I grew up amid the ripples from that time, the Pol Pot era of my parents' generation. The blood of my ancestors boils in my veins, and so does yours. As you're reading this book, you're not sitting there by yourself. You are carrying genes dating back countless generations, from people whose genes mixed with those of others and mutated along the way. A long line of people behind us paved the way for us to be here right now. If you can't find any other force to be grateful for, be grateful for that. Maybe your great-grandmother tripped and the man who would become your great-grandfather happened to be nearby and helped her up. They looked into each other's eyes and fell in love – and 120 years later, here you are! Coincidence? Maybe. But I'd like to persuade you to believe that something like that has happened for each and every one of us, because if it hadn't, we wouldn't be here.

TIPS AND TOOLS

- **Write down your Spiritual Foundation goal for the day.** Find an action you can take that will make you feel connected, if not to God, then to others; and if not to others, then to yourself. Ask, *What's my gut telling me? Am I anxious? Am I sad?* Like a second brain, the gut is worth listening to. Your intention for the day for the Spiritual Foundation might be taking three to four minutes to sit or lie quietly and to tune into what your gut is telling you. Perhaps it's to pray or do a guided five-minute meditation. Maybe your goal for the day will be something like, "Today

Foundation 4: Spiritual

I will message my friend X and tell them I love them". Or "Hi Jenny, I really appreciate that you dropped by yesterday and asked how I was doing. It meant a lot to me." Plain, simple and authentic, this type of message will help you build connections with people.

- **Practise gratitude.** Gratitude is about appreciating things and giving them your attention.

    » Begin by noticing the good things that happen to you or that you see around you, anything from beauty in nature to touching human moments. Look for them, appreciate them and feel the warm glow they give you.

    » Start a gratitude journal and make it a regular practice to appreciate good things from your day.

    » Express your gratitude towards yourself and others: when someone has been there for you when you needed them, for example, or when someone has done a job well. Either write it down or say it out loud. Thank someone by sending them a note or flowers, or take them for a coffee and tell them how and why you're grateful for them.

    » Meditate or pray, reflecting on what you are grateful for in your life.

    » Take a walk in which you appreciate everything good around you.

    » Practise mindful eating. Be present as you eat, and appreciate the nourishment you're receiving.

- **Dance.** Put on tribal music, shake and shimmy your hips and tap into the energy of your ancestors. Trauma is stored in the hips, and this is one reason our ancestors did tribal dancing – to shake off generational trauma. I invite you to bring that practice back into your life: shaking off the low energy and getting in touch with your spine is a way of regulating your nervous system. Why not take off all your clothes and dance alone naked in your room? Go on, I dare you! Own the body you were born in, appreciate the heart that's beating for you, the lungs that are breathing for you even when you're sleeping, the legs that move you. Be grateful for this body you have.

- **Meditate for five or ten minutes.** I do ten-minute meditations using the Calm app. The Headspace app is excellent too. Meditation is about sitting quietly and not judging your thoughts. While there are many methods available, the idea is to simply watch your thoughts come and then let them go. Don't try to suppress your thoughts or stop negativity. Let the negative thoughts happen; you are just a doorframe with a camera that lets things pass through it and observes it all.

Try a gratitude meditation, putting your hands on your heart and counting all the blessings in your life. I have my own rituals and your own will probably evolve over time. I cross my hands over my heart in a butterfly shape and think about my daughter, my home, my friends, the water I drink. You can even highlight specific events: "Jenny came to visit me yesterday; she didn't have to drop by my office and ask me how I'm doing, but she did. She spent five minutes listening to my problems and I'm so grateful for her."

I then go into my EMDR: Eye Movement Desensitisation and Reprocessing, a psychotherapy treatment that helps

Foundation 4: Spiritual

alleviate the distress associated with traumatic memories. If you are interested, consult a therapist who is trained in this modality, as it's very helpful for inner child healing. During the process you are taken to a state in which you feel safe, then you physically tap yourself with your fingers, which rewires your brain to associate a particular experience with the pleasant emotion. When I think of my traumatic experience from childhood, it no longer triggers the old feelings and I feel safe.

- **Join classes and groups to support your journey.** Look up a spiritual or religious group you're interested in and approach them. Usually these events are free; be curious and go along. There might not be a religion that suits you but, equally, there might be one that does.

You will emerge from this as the person you were meant to be.

We will all meet our end one day, and it's what we think of in our dying moments that matters the most. It'll never be wishing that you'd redecorated your living room or not skipped that day of work. At the end, you will reflect on what you loved, mostly people, and the good you did and the people you helped during your life.

Don't get me wrong – private jets, Lamborghinis and other expensive material goods are made to be enjoyed, and it's fine to use them guilt-free. Yet when you're on your deathbed you won't be thinking about your Lamborghini or your private jet. (The truth is that your first private jet experience might be fantastic, but it gets old by the twentieth time.) What you will think about is the significant moments in your life, and those moments are only memorable and meaningful because they are shared with others. You can make a million dollars, but if you're the only one with a million and everyone around you is poor and suffering, you won't be making great memories. I've gathered knowledge from a whole host of amazing people around the world, by reading books written by them, listening to them speak, being coached by them, attending their seminars and hosting seminars for them. I've had the opportunity to be in the same room as these highly successful billionaires, and they all come to the same conclusion: money means nothing if you have no one worthwhile to share it with. Fulfilment is intertwined with the people in your life and the positive influence you have on them. We explored the importance of authentic relationships in the previous chapter. Now understand that you need those people to share amazing moments with when you've made your money! (We'll explore how in the next chapter, Foundation 5: Financial.)

Your life becomes well rounded when there is a higher purpose attached to the dollars you make. Your days are no longer meaningless. And there will be a fine line between what you're willing to compromise on and what you're not.

Consider a model having to keep in shape for work. Sounds vain, right? But what if she's doing it to support herself through school, or even to support her family? Suddenly that sacrifice seems reasonable, even purposeful. Now step this up further and imagine that this model has gone through significant trauma. She's now successful and famous, and is no longer motivated by the sheer need to survive. Now she's working for a cause – to help others through the sorts of traumatic experiences that hurt her.

When you're vibrating at a higher frequency, you no longer do things just for yourself; you do them for the collective good. When

Foundation 4: Spiritual

it's just you, it's meaningless, and I tell you this from experience.

Find your purpose. I'm starting a podcast because I'm hungry for knowledge and I want to empower women. I'm writing a book because I want to help women get out of their rut, get back on their feet, follow their dreams and do something good for themselves. This is my motto: *I want to be so happy that God uses my light to shine on others, and I want to be so rich that God uses my pocket to bless others.* I'm not doing this for me; I'm doing this because I've been given a greater purpose.

This is my second life. As you know, six years ago I came very close to taking my own life, but after experiencing faith that fateful night, I had to reevaluate my life: rip the rug out from under my feet and rearrange everything because what I'd been doing wasn't working. If you aren't in that dark space, I'm happy for you. If you are, you have my absolute sympathy, my deepest love and care, and I am sending you faith, love and light. Believe that there is something out there conspiring for you to travel this journey so you can come out the other side the highest version of yourself – the person you are meant to be. You will be unleashed, as I was.

I was born with a vision to help other women break free from their conditioning and generational curses. To me, it feels as if that's written in my DNA. Of course I have the choice of whether or not to activate that vision – and I'm choosing to do it. The vision and the mission were given to me, and I am fortunate that I've opened myself up enough to be able to hear these voices. I listen to what is true to me. Ask yourself, "What is true for me?"… and wait, listening for the answer.

Foundation 5: Financial

Believe that you are worthy of money.

You might not believe this but I used to be broke, and it was because I had a really bad relationship with money. What I learned from my experience is that in order to attract wealth into our lives, we need to heal our relationship with money, so we feel worthy of it and start operating from a place of abundance instead of a place of lack.

Open up your mind and think about the kind of lifestyle you want. Currently you might go to work at 9 a.m. and finish at 5 p.m., and then you need to get ready for tomorrow again – but for what? Paying bills, of course. This way of being has been imposed on us by the "system". Many people love to be in the system because it's familiar and feels safe. And you can buy a house! Buy a second house, buy a third house! The big dream for many of us is to own property, which is great – but if you never break out of the system, you remain a slave.

To me, quality of life is not a matter of wealth; it's a matter of freedom. You can have a billion dollars, but if you work 20 hours a day and don't have time to spend with loved ones or the freedom to pursue your interests, you are a slave. To me, what matters is

Foundation 5: Financial

how free you are in what you do.

That said, everyone needs resources. I don't care if you tell me money can't buy you happiness. Imagine having money to spare, enough to pay off your mother's mortgage and then to splurge. How would that feel? Pretty good, I imagine! Or I'll give you $1,000,000 so you can fly your parents or your siblings or your best friend to Paris first class and then watch how happy they are when they eat croissants and drink champagne while flying above the clouds. If that's not what happiness looks like for you, then think about other ways money can bring you joy.

I love money and money loves me, and the reason this happened is because I healed my connection with money – an extremely powerful step. To get started, let's look at the amount you feel you deserve. Everybody has a number, a threshold for where they feel their money should be. This is their comfortable place, whether $5,000 or $50,000. For different people it's a different amount of money; for some it might be just $5. When you see that number in your bank account, you feel good, but as soon as your bank balance goes below that, you start to feel anxious: "Aaargh, I must do something about this! I'm dipping into my savings and that's bad. I need to work harder. Where can I find more income?"

None of this is intentional, of course. You don't decide to make a certain number your threshold. You don't say to yourself, "Hmm, alright, $30,000 is my number", for example. Of course you'd rather have $100,000! For about ten years I was well off financially and didn't have to worry about money. During that time, the amount I felt I should always have in the bank was $30,000. That was what I believed I was worthy of, and that was a comfortable amount considering my lifestyle and expenses. Also, I liked that number because it was what I was used to. People's numbers

Good Girl

vary greatly according to circumstances. If you're a housewife whose expenses are low because your husband is taking care of your bills, then having $20,000 or $30,000 in your account as your cushion might be plenty. But if you want to change your lifestyle, your number might look very different.

I think of the threshold amount as how much money a person feels they deserve. In this way, money is linked to our sense of self-worth – and we can change that. We can work on grasping what we're worthy of. So, let's raise that bar and see what happens. If your current threshold is $10,000, let's move the needle to, say, $20,000. Naturally, it will take work to get there, but I'm here to tell you that it is possible. After years of sitting at $30,000, I read a few books about money and started thinking differently. I asked myself, "How much money do I feel I deserve? How much money do I want?" I thought, *I want half a million dollars.* And somehow, it happened.

But be warned: money can turn tail and go away again. Once you step out of your comfort zone, the person who's used to that safety will be pulling you back! In addition, managing $500,000 requires different knowledge and skills than what's needed for managing $10,000, including new accounting and investment strategies. More money means more responsibility. Now you'll have to invest the money you have, pay tax on it, manage it responsibly. It's almost easier to spend it all and become broke again! Which is what many people do. So, I had two options when I started wanting to attract more money: either I could level up to match the energy of $500,000 or I could stay at $30,000 in my thinking and my skills.

Eventually most people will return to their old threshold, which is why many lottery-winners lose everything within a few years and go back to where they were financially. They lack

Foundation 5: Financial

the energetic vibration and financial literacy to align with the amount of money they won. Being broke is what they are used to, so when they get a windfall they will keep drifting back down to their baseline of what feels comfortable. Because their needle is set at a particular number, they feel subconsciously driven to splurge and blow that new money, and it's gone as fast as it's come in. Many years ago, my threshold used to be $10,000: if my bank balance dipped below that, I'd think, "Oh no, I've got to find jobs and new projects!" If it was above $50,000, I'd think, "Oo, maybe I'll go buy a Gucci belt or a new phone..."

Opening yourself to more money is as much about educating yourself as it is about changing your mindset and your vibration around money to match a higher amount. Maybe you don't think you deserve $500,000. Maybe you don't think you're worthy enough to invest that money and multiply it. And that's an important point, because the second you don't think you're worthy of something, it's gone, *whoosh*, just like that.

You may ask me, "Hey, Piyané, if we're all on top, who's going to be at the bottom?" The truth is that there's plenty of room up here for everyone, to be financially free. There's enough resources on the planet for every person. "But still," you say, "if everyone is rich, who is poor?" Money is all around us. Do billionaires keep their money stashed under the mattress or locked away in a safe? No, those billions of dollars are out there in circulation, flowing around as trades, exchanges, stocks, bonds, private equity, e-commerce purchases and more. As you are reading, there are billions of dollars being traded invisibly online, bank deposits and lease payments being made, and stocks getting bought and sold. All we need is a channel to open up so the money can drop down onto us. Money comes to us when we're equal to that energy – when we believe we're worthy of that money. If you're a

Good Girl

freelancer and don't think your work is good enough, how much do you charge? Not enough, for sure. You have to elevate your mindset to match the amount you want. If you're thinking, "I'm not smart enough to earn more," perhaps you've simply had a bad relationship with money until now, and the good news is that can be changed.

What is your number? Think about it, write it down, then let's work with it. I know this may sound strange, but stay with me. When you move the needle a bit, your brain will start thinking differently. For example, you might see that if you're working 9 to 5, only making money by selling your services during those hours and not earning money in your sleep, you'll be working until the day you die. You will be a slave to time. If you fall ill or something befalls you, money will stop coming in. Of course I'm not telling you to quit your job, but I want you to know that your money should be working just as hard as you are to make money for you.

How to make this happen is something you'll have to discover for yourself. Some people are interested in stocks, for instance, others in property development, ecommerce or real estate.

If you have a job as a copywriter, consider starting a side hustle making use of that expertise. What resources do you have? Perhaps you could gather a team who work overseas for you part-time. For example, I'm Cambodian and use a lot of contractors for design work. These excellent designers don't charge as much as their counterparts in other countries, so I could create my own business where customers pay me a surcharge and I act as middle-person between them and these designers. The designers get well-paid work, I charge the customer for my knowledge of how to unite these two markets, and everyone benefits. Plus, I could create an app and a website, taking this business to the point where I don't even have to be involved in

Foundation 5: Financial

it any more. You might know this concept – it's like the platform Fiver, but on a smaller scale.

How can you sell your skills? If you're good at sourcing, on weekends you could help a small business source goods like tote bags. Do it well enough and you could create your own website and list on Alibaba or Amazon. Read up on online shopping and trading and start building up your knowledge and confidence.

That first person who became rich in a line of wealthy people probably worked their butt off to get the skills and know-how they needed, and that's what we're aiming for too. Looking around my desk, I see my handbag, my camera, a plastic bag, a water bottle – every single thing that is man-made was once a thought in someone's head. Somebody said, "I wish I could..." and started to make that product. If you can think it, you can create it. And, if you can think of the amount of money you want and ways to go about making the money, you can make that happen too. The only difference between people who've already done it and you, is the will to do it. Action is what counts. You can dream it, but if you do nothing about it, nothing happens. My advice to you is to *just start*. And believe that you're worthy of wealth and success.

- A dream without a plan is just a fantasy.
- A dream with steps but no timeline is a loose plan.
- A dream with plans and a realistic timeline is commitment.
- A dream with plans, a realistic timeline and consistent action becomes a reality.

I failed at multiple businesses but that didn't stop me. I wouldn't be where I am today if I hadn't gone through all that and learned from what I did. Think about it: if the inventor of the lightbulb gave up on the thirtieth try, we wouldn't have artificial light today. We wouldn't have handbags or chairs or toilets if someone hadn't kept going. So, the will to take consistent action is crucial for financial freedom. It's not going to be easy, and often you will feel uncomfortable, sitting in a room where people are discussing things you don't understand. *What is tax? What is R&D? What are stocks? What is a mortgage bond? What is liquidity?* You might be sitting there feeling stupid and overwhelmed, but you need to take action. Find a way to educate yourself: learn about money and business and find someone to mentor you who has succeeded financially themselves. Learn from other people who have already done what you want to do, then model them.

It's likely that you have a skill to sell. Say you're a wedding photographer with a top-notch camera and you sell your time by photographing weddings on weekends. How can you make multiple income streams from this skill? Let's think... you could create your own filters or presets for creative photo effects and sell those online. Or create a filters package and sell it online on Shopify, for example (there are plenty of YouTube tutorials to show you how). Customers can click a button online to buy your filters for $30 and pay you while you're sleeping! Sell 50 of those a week and that's $1,500. Free money! Also, there are potential customers out there who want to be wedding photographers like you, who are willing to spend money learning how – and they'd much rather learn from someone who's already a successful photographer than go to university and take a course on the history of film. Upload your portfolio and for $1,000 you can teach these eager people the ins and outs of wedding photography: lighting, lenses, editing techniques. It took you ten years to learn your craft and you're giving them a crash course so they can become skilled in a fraction of the time. Just think, you could run

Foundation 5: Financial

a workshop for $200 a head; if 100 people sign up, that's $20,000 in your pocket! Or teach on YouTube. In this online age, the world is your audience.

Even if you have no plans to leave your job, let's turn our attention to your savings and how to expand them. If you love your job and are good at it, you might well have a certain amount of savings ready to invest. By the way, there are two reasons why you'll stay in a job: either it's teaching you something or it's paying you well. If you have no savings, you're probably staying because you have no money management skills. This can be a direct result of not feeling worthy of having money, Money may even intimidate you.

Perhaps you feel you don't have much financial knowledge; in that case, write down in your journal for today's Foundation 5 goal, "Spend fifteen minutes googling or ask around for a good financial advisor". Or talk to a wealthy person in your circle who knows how to invest and makes good decisions with their money. Ask them questions; they are very likely to share with you the techniques, the people, the resources, seminars and books that helped them acquire their investment knowledge. They probably won't tell you exactly *how* they're investing their money and who they're investing it with, though, which is fair enough. But when your wealthy contact gives you a lead, follow that lead. Tomorrow, as your Foundation 5 goal, schedule fifteen minutes to do exactly that. If the lead is a dead-end or doesn't work out, think of other ways you can spend your Foundation 5 time. You don't necessarily have to invest to make money. Have dinner conversations with wealthy people and later google any terms they mention with which you aren't familiar. Read up and keep learning.

Do you have any hobbies you can monetise? You might be a

Good Girl

good human resources manager, but you might also be a spear-fisherman on the side. Let's brainstorm how you can monetise that hobby – by making videos of yourself spear-fishing and sharing them on YouTube and Facebook? Try whichever avenue feels right to you. If you're a stay-at-home mother with zero savings and no hobby you're passionate about, or you've just left an abusive relationship and have no extra money, what now? Google something new that intrigues you. Learn a new skill from YouTube videos. Let's set the intention to find a hobby that earns you money. When you're doing something you enjoy that makes you money, it doesn't feel like work. And if you have the will to do it, there's always a way. Fifteen minutes a day of googling your idea is the bare minimum to start your journey.

You might say, "So, googling something for fifteen minutes a day is your big idea, then?" My response is an exasperated "*YES!*", because people *don't* do this. Or they get lost in that vast search engine because there's a deluge of information out there. Do a fifteen-minute targeted search today, then repeat tomorrow but go in deeper. Or spend that time making calls to various people who could help you improve your finance and investment knowledge and skills. Keep doing that, and you'll be amazed by what you will achieve.

Seven years ago, I didn't know a thing about starting a cosmetics company. I knew ingredients that worked from my years of doing reviews for skin-care brands, but by no means am I an expert chemist. I didn't know which manufacturer to choose or which grants I might eligible for. Where do you think I learned all of this to begin with? Google, of course! That then prompted me to ask basic questions that sometimes made me feel like an idiot... but that's how Nalia Cosmetics was born! We all have to start somewhere.

Foundation 5: Financial

I also googled how to stop being depressed, and one website led me to another. It advised, "get a life coach" so I googled that. Then I joined a support group and asked around: had anyone there worked with a life coach they'd recommend? Someone gave me a name, and I have now worked with this life-changing coach for seven years. My coach said to me, "You are definitely a coach. You are an author. You should write a book." There I was, mumbling about not being good enough, but she kept encouraging me, so I googled "how to write a book" and found someone to help me with that too. And here we are, together in the pages of this book.

TIPS AND TOOLS

- **List your Financial Foundation goal for the day.** In five or ten minutes, how can you explore making an extra stream of income today? How can you make multiple streams of income? Perhaps it's to learn something new. You might list as your goal listening to five minutes of a financial podcast or reading two pages of a book about managing your money or investing. Google something that has piqued your interest: cryptocurrency or private equity, for example. Or, if you're considering switching jobs in order to earn more, google ways to upskill yourself. AI is rich with opportunity: could you explore something like Canva, the free AI image generator, to bring in extra income?
- **Create a vision board.** Gather some magazines and cut out pictures that represent experiences, items and feelings you want, then stick them on some cardboard and keep your vision board in a place where you will see it often. I used to keep my vision board in my bedroom. Now

Good Girl

that you have a board full of the things you're aiming for, you won't feel guilty when you get them; it will feel more like an achievement. You're not vain for wanting a Chanel bag – you deserve it. You're worthy of it. You're working hard for it. Why feel guilty?

- **Read books about money.** I recommend *Rich Dad Poor Dad* by Robert Kiyosaki.[29] Pick up a few books on how to invest: *The Barefoot Investor* by Scott Pape[30] is a good start.
- **Write a brutally honest letter to money.** Get a piece of paper and start writing to money right now. It's likely that some icky stuff will come out! This exercise will reveal to you your current relationship with money. Write "Dear Money", and then open up the floodgates. Be completely honest. For many people the letter might read:

    Dear Money,
    I hate you… I need you but you're never there for me
    You're so X, Y and Z. etc.

- **Write a gratitude letter to money.** Something I like to do is write about what money does for me. For example, we lack good medical facilities in Cambodia, so I will often take my parents to Thailand or Singapore for treatment. Afterwards, I'll write in my journal how thankful I am for the money I was able to use to take care of their health.

---

[29] Robert T. Kiyosaki, *Rich Dad Poor Dad: What the Rich Teach Their Kids About Money That the Poor and Middle Class Do Not!* (Plata Publishing: 2017).

[30] Scott Pape, *The Barefoot Investor: The Only Money Guide You'll Ever Need* (Wiley: 2020).

Foundation 5: Financial

Something else I wrote about in a gratitude letter to money was the time I bought my very own first-class ticket to Dubai, something which had been on my bucket list. I had to forgo buying a particular item so I could afford the ticket, and I thought, "Yes, this is a once-in-a-lifetime experience I want to have." I wrote about how I had enjoyed every sip of my drinks, savoured all the details and special touches, and had appreciated not having to wait in a long queue to board or exit the plane. I did not feel guilty one bit – which demonstrates a good relationship with money. Money can buy you comfort and a sense of love for yourself. It brings the feeling of someone else pampering you, only it's you.

Let's pause here and talk a bit about judging others' spending. Do you find it disgusting that someone could own an $8,000 handbag, for example? Would you say, "There are so many people out there starving and you're buying a purse!"? If that thought occurs to you, it merely means you have a bad relationship with money. People operate within their ratio and it's all relative. While this sort of spending might seem excessive to you, it isn't to others. The proportion of money I spend on helping others is also a lot higher, as is the amount I pay in taxes. Consider this: you spending a few hundred dollars on a handbag would seem equally ridiculous to someone living in rural Cambodia. They'd look at you, stupefied, and say, "You spent $300 on a *bag*?" They've never seen $300 in their life!

If you feel appalled by how other people spend their money, it is merely a reflection of your relationship with money. Other people's money is theirs, not yours, and how they choose to spend it is up to them. What's it to you? Do you scroll through social media and hate seeing rich people going about their luxury-filled lives? If so, the reason you hate it so much is that you have a love-hate relationship with money. You can't live without it, but when you have it you probably feel anxious and don't know how to deal with it.

For me, buying an $8,000 handbag is a way of gifting myself, because gift-giving is one of my love languages. For you, signs of achievement might be buying a car or a house or having a mortgage. But I've paid off my mortgage and I have a car, and that $8,000 bag is something I really wanted, so don't judge me. Take my Chanel bag away from me and I'm still Piyané. This bag is simply something I use and like, and it demonstrates my ratio: how much money I make and how much money I can spare. Also, I didn't take from the money I use for charity work and helping others to buy this bag. You don't know what anyone does behind the scenes, so don't judge anyone for the bag they're carrying. Instead, I invite you to look within yourself. Does your judgment come from a sense of lack?

Now you know I own some cute bags. But when I go home, all my furniture has been bought from Facebook Marketplace and Ikea. From tables and chairs to my desk, my items of furniture tend to cost around $100 each. I'm simply used to buying these things from such outlets and it has never occurred to me to try anything different. Again, a $100 table is very expensive for someone living in poverty in Cambodia or any other country. Also, you might be happily using Ikea furniture right now and

Foundation 5: Financial

thinking, "What is she saying? I love my Ikea stuff!" If so, that's great. But then I went to my friend's place. She's a hairdresser and doesn't make loads of money, but she has a very nice, expensive couch. It cost $5,000, whereas I have $300 couches in my apartment. I went over to her couch, stroked the leather, plopped down on it… Aaahhh… it felt amazing! "How did you afford this couch?" I asked her, thinking I couldn't afford one. She looked at me quizzically at the time; seven years ago now. "Isn't that a Chanel bag?" she asked. "That's $8,000 dollars sitting right there. And you have a couple of them! Just don't buy one bag – then you'll be able to buy a couch."

At that moment, I realised, "Yes! I *can* afford a couch like this." It was all about my mindset. Up to that point, I had thought I could only afford Ikea furniture and second-hand items from Facebook Marketplace. But then I realised I just needed to stop buying a bag here and a pair of shoes there, and then I'd be able to buy a good couch I can sit comfortably on. This "aha" moment opened up my mind about my restrictive feelings around money – and not only that, but every other area of my life where I was stuck and my threshold was low.

Get out of a mindset of lack and into a mindset of abundance.

Has there ever been a bill you've urgently had to pay? Have you ever had to pay the rent or you'd be kicked out of your house, or got a flat tyre and had to buy a new one so you could get to work? Somehow you came up with the money. I know you did. You sold your shoes, you borrowed from someone: wherever it came from, somehow that money materialised. And you manifested it

Good Girl

because that's who you are. You never attract what you want; you attract *who you are* – and at that moment you were someone who had to get from A to B and needed that car to run or that rent to be paid.

Let's expand this idea. If you need or want something badly enough because that's who you are, you will manifest it. All the other Foundations we've worked through have helped you create a picture of who you are, down to the details. In Physical, how do you want to look? What do you want to eat? Where do you want to spend your time? In Mental & Emotional, what do you want to read? What kind of content do you want to consume? What type of feeling state do you want to be in? In Community, what kind of people do you want to hang out with? And now Financial: how are you going to support all of this? You can have all the other four Foundations, but when you have the abundance of the Financial Foundation, it will take you to the next level.

Regardless of what you might think, we need money in this world. Wanting money doesn't make you greedy. Money isn't bad. If I tell you I can afford a first-class plane ticket and your first thought is, "That's disgusting! You shouldn't be living that way," it means your relationship with money needs work because you don't identify as someone who can afford first class. Even though you might want it deep-down, you justify your reluctance to embrace it as something noble, saying, "I'd rather spend it on charity." I don't fly first class all the time, by the way – I often travel economy class. But if the very words "first class" trigger a strong reaction in you, it means that something within you rejects the fact that you are worthy of sitting there.

Why do you hate that idea so much, and whose idea is it? It might in fact not be your idea at all, but simply a result of the environment you grew up in. Perhaps poverty was the norm during

Foundation 5: Financial

your upbringing; perhaps not being able to afford the rent or to eat at a nice restaurant was normal – but is this something you want for your future? Is this what you desire for your best self? For your children and your family? If it isn't, then I invite you to explore what it is about money that icks you out. What is it that makes you roll your eyes when that asshole around the corner starts revving his Lamborghini? Why do you see someone dressed up to the nines and think, "That's so snobby"? Why can't you and these other people happily coexist? They are merely choosing to spend their life in a different way.

Other people are a mirror. The reason you don't like money is probably because you don't have any, plain and simple. You may think you know better, but all you might know is poverty and having people around you who need money. You might think you have a better idea of how to spend those millions or billions – pay off your mother's mortgage, support charities, donate to an orphanage etc – and if that's the case, wouldn't it be better if that money was in your pocket? If your income was so great that you had $500,000 to splurge, what would you spend it on? And would you feel guilty about it? Because if you feel guilty spending money on yourself, you are broke. You'll never meet a financially successful person who feels guilty spending money on themselves, because they know that *they* are the best investment they can make.

Why do successful people have private jets? I know many billionaires who fly on private jets, and it's not because they want to splurge. They don't even post pictures online about it! The reason they do it is to save time. At this stage of their lives, the most valuable resource is no longer money but time. They don't want to waste their time queuing; they just want to get from A to B as quickly as possible because they have back-to-back

Good Girl

meetings. As an example, today I woke up at 6 a.m. and had an event till 10 a.m. Then I had a meeting at 12, a meeting at 12.30, a meeting at 1 that finished at 3, then a meeting at 3.30 that finished at 5, and now I have another meeting. If I had to fly to Singapore or Thailand for another appointment later, wouldn't it be better for my physical and mental well-being to charter a private plane to get there? I think so. It's not that these people are so rich that they've lost touch with the rest of humanity; it's that time is now their most important resource.

My goal at this point in my life is to empower people, but I don't want the stress of sitting cramped for eleven hours in an economy seat and then having to get straight off the plane and give a speech. Does the fact that I wish to sit in business class mean I'm showing off? No, it means I want to be comfortable as I work on my life purpose. I'm confident enough to say that my values aren't about sacrificing my own comfort so that I can be seen by others as a humble person. I live comfortably because I have a higher purpose to serve. I use the resources I have wisely, and that includes my time.

The first time I went on a plane was at age eleven. We were travelling to Thailand, only an hour's flight from Cambodia, and I remember walking onto the plane towards our seats with my parents and my sister. It was a small flight; no first class section, only business class and economy. As we filed past the business class section, I said to my parents, "These are bigger seats. Why aren't we sitting here?" My father said, "Huh, this section is for rich people only." I said, "What? We're not rich?" I couldn't believe it! At that age, I'd never mixed with wealthy people, only with my cousins, my aunts and uncles and my parents. Only acquainted with my own community, I didn't even know what wealth looked like.

Foundation 5: Financial

A few years later, once I'd started making money working as a DJ, among other jobs, I began posting on MySpace (for younger readers, MySpace was like an early version of Facebook) and I saw posts by rich kids who were flying first class and business class. I thought, "Wow, that's unrealistic for me. I'm just a DJ getting paid fuck-all. That's impossible for me." That's when I got bitter and built a bad relationship with money. I told myself, "I can't get there; that's for rich people only. Those spoilt kids are splurging and I'm here working my butt off and I'm not even getting the respect I need!" I was young and didn't know any better.

Then you move up in life and there's always the next mountain to climb, isn't there? When you've never flown before, you think, "Oh, I just want to go on a plane!" Next, it's "Oh! I want to sit in business class." And when you're sitting in business class, you think, "Ah, look at first class over there. Wouldn't that be wonderful?" And when you're in first class, a few fellow passengers will say to you, "Oh, well, I'm going to my next appointment on my private jet," and you'll think, "There are private jets?!" There's always something bigger and better out there, and you can level up or you can remain comfortable. Yes, it's nice being comfortable where you are, but comfort is where your dreams go to die. I started being exposed to people flying business class and first class and eating at nice restaurants. Then I had a choice: either I could step higher or I could secretly resent the belief that I would never be able to enjoy a lifestyle like that.

Picture me at age seventeen and eighteen, a girl who loved eating Western food like steak. In Cambodia we eat rice daily and your meals would cost between $2 to $3 per day, an amount that could buy you a good restaurant meal. But in the Western restaurants, a meal would cost $15 – a lot of money for me at the time. That said, even if I only had $20 in my pocket, I would go to

Good Girl

eat at a nice restaurant. I'd sit and pore over the menu, gaze at all the lovely things around me, and then I'd order something that only cost $10, plus another $2 of drinks. In total, the experience would cost me about $12 – almost half of my spending money. I know this isn't a sensible money strategy, but it exposed me to a lifestyle I'd had no access to while growing up. I'd only seen restaurants and meals like these on TV and thought, "Oh, I want to try that too!"

TV host and producer Steve Harvey said something along these lines: every single person should buy a first class plane ticket and eat at a fancy restaurant because it exposes you to different things and elevates your mindset. If you discover you hate those experiences, that's fine, but if you like them you can start to aim for something better. If all you know is poverty, you'll have the opportunity to break your generational curse. You might think all those rich people out there are only going to marry rich people and help each other get wealthier – but the thing is, even if there's a long line of rich people, someone had to get rich in the first place. How did they do that? This is your invitation to become that person.

Generational wealth is cyclic. Life is all about cycles, and once we figure out how it works, we can hack our life. War and peace happen in cycles too, and generations who've endured hardship go on to create abundance: because they've experienced tough conditions, they are driven to make a world of peace and plenty for everyone and give their children everything they can. And then, by doing so, they inadvertently create a weak generation of sensitive kids who've grown up cushioned by abundance. The weak generation will go on to stir up problems, which will bring forth a new generation of hard people. These tough types will go on to create abundance and wealth, which will produce a new

Foundation 5: Financial

generation of weak people. And so on.

As soon as you realise the cyclical nature of society and civilisation, you'll see that your hardship is a good thing. It means you are tough and resilient and you have perseverance. You've overcome your difficulties and are not easily bent. You are a survivor! Use this to your advantage. The fact that you aren't going to be offended or hurt as easily as someone who's had a more cushioned existence will help you in life, because rejection is part of the program. The worst thing that can happen when you try something new is that you get humiliated. What happens next is that those who witnessed your screw-up move on to the next thing. It's over. Think of Kim Kardashian's leaked sex tape – she benefited greatly from it. People may have loved it or hated it, but do you think she cares? She has a whole empire behind her, and businesspeople like her turn bad situations into good ones.

If mentioning the Kardashians and their savvy business strategies triggers something negative in you, I again invite you to look inside yourself. What is it about yourself that you don't like that is mirrored by them? The truth is that you cannot like or dislike something you don't identify with. For example, if I walk down the road and see an ugly tree, I'm not going to be offended by it – I have nothing in common with it. If I see a funny-looking raccoon dancing on the street, I will probably laugh because it mirrors me. It's dancing, shaking its booty, and I like that. I'll think, "Ah, that raccoon has my sense of humour." You have to identify with something for it to generate emotion.

So, back to that guy round the corner in his Lamborghini, wearing his Louis Vuitton tracksuit and honking his horn and looking like a jackass. What is it about his displays of wealth that trigger you so much? Go beyond the hatred and see it for what it is: it's about your bad relationship with money.

Good Girl

If you say it's because he's obnoxious and his honking horn or revved-up motor is disturbing your peace, I invite you to picture a guy with a beaten-up car, revving his engine and honking his horn. Do you have the same reaction of disgust, or do you just feel annoyed? The difference is that the guy in the Lamborghini is displaying things you lack – money, self-assurance, and freedom from financial worries about the future. It feels disgusting to you because he is flaunting what you don't have.

Perhaps you don't like money or you identify it as bad. Or you believe people with money are assholes. But there are plenty of people out there with money who are good people, and if you believe you are a good person, isn't money better in your pocket? So why are you feeling guilty for wanting a billion dollars, or a million dollars, or 20 million? And let me ask you something else: why do you want that money? What's it going to be used for? If you have a genuine purpose for your money, then you won't lose it; if not, you'll be like those lottery winners and quickly go broke because your threshold is low. You need a *reason* to have all that money in your bank account.

To be a functioning member of society you need money, regardless of whether you're a man or a woman. Otherwise, how are you going to help your family? Contribute in a meaningful way? Experience life? How are you going to provide for your son and daughter and support your parents? Build a house? Get from A to B? Everyone can be rich, every single person. Money is zooming all around us in transactions; you just need to open up a little channel so the money can drop into your lap. You need to be set at the right frequency for this to happen – the way you can't have your radio set at AM if you want to listen to music on FM. You need to learn the language of money and understand it: read up on it, google terms you've heard, attend seminars, listen

Foundation 5: Financial

to podcasts. Improve your knowledge and try something new.

I am not a financial advisor but I'm sharing my experiences with you so that you can learn from them. Identifying yourself with the amount of money you have will make it very hard for you to invest because you'll struggle to make decisions. You'll never want to take a financial risk; you will wait until something is a sure thing before you take action, and that means never acting or acting far too late. Take it from me, someone who's failed at many businesses and at some point thought she had lost everything... When you take no risk at all, your money will decline and decline. For me, success is when I look at money and I don't see money any more; I see an asset. My money is not my identity. My money is neither good nor bad. Money in itself is neutral – it is simply a resource.

Emotional detachment is a useful mindset to have around money. To illustrate this, imagine I'm hiring someone to work for me. If that person happens to be my cousin or nephew, I'll feel emotionally attached to them, which means I'm likely to overlook their mistakes and will spend time trying to guide them. If, however, I hire a complete stranger, I will regard them as an asset and a resource in my company; I will be able to evaluate their performance and make decisions soundly because this individual isn't attached to me and my identity. Of course I'll treat them with respect, love, care and compassion, but in a professional manner.

You should be treating your money the same way. If you see your money the way you see your cousins, nephews and nieces, you will make decisions emotionally rather than rationally. Detaching yourself from money doesn't mean going out and splurging; like hiring an employee, you must take care of your resources. What it does mean is that you should make your decisions about your money logically, not emotionally.

Good Girl

How rich do you want to be?

Think of the universe and how things manifest. Everything around us that's man-made, someone once thought of. They *thought* of it before it was made. So, you can do the same in your life. If you want a million dollars to manifest in your life, you need the vibration to match that million dollars. Imagine I'm a genie and you say me, "Help me, genie, I want to be rich. I want to be free. How do I do it?" (I have a lot of conversations with people who ask me things like this.)

"Okay, so you want to be rich," I say. "How rich?"

"I want a few million dollars," you say.

"Okay, a few million dollars. What for?"

Now, this is where most people can't answer the question. They probably want to pay off their mortgage, pay off their debt, pay off a credit card – but that's thinking from a place of lack, not abundance. If you go to a bank and tell them you want to borrow some money, they'll ask, "How much do you want?" If you reply, "I want to be rich. I want to pay off my debts," how likely is it that the bank will give you the money?

But say you approach them with a plan like this: "I have an opportunity to invest! I found this opening and here is my collateral. I also have this asset over here. Give me $3,000,000 to invest" (or $400,000, or $200,000, or whatever amount you need). You'll see the difference in the response from the bank. The universe works the same way. You can't just show up and say, "I want to be rich." How rich? Give an exact number. And what's the money for? If you are clear about the purpose of that money, you're more likely to get it.

This concept can be applied to absolutely everything you desire in your life. You don't want to be depressed any more? All right, then what *do* you want? If your answer is "I want to be

Foundation 5: Financial

happy", then how happy? You might say, "I don't want to be in debt any more. I don't like my job. I hate my life. My mother is a problem. I hate my father-in-law." Yeah, yeah, yeah. You already know what's not right in your life, but you're not doing anything about it and you're asking to be happy. How can you get there? What are the tools that will help? Well, you can avoid those problem people in your life and then work on yourself, so get started.

Be brutally honest with yourself: are you really happy with your financial situation? If your answer is "Yes, I have a good relationship with money and the amount I have is enough", why are you reading my book? Go out there and eat croissants and enjoy your life! If not, be willing to ask for help. There are two things we are never taught – how to have sex and how to make money – and yet we are expected to be good at both. These are taboo topics, never discussed, but we're expected to ace them. To improve, we need to break stigmas and talk about taboos like money. My advice to you is to be bold, be brave, take your power back and ask questions. Be willing to look like an idlot. As I've said, embarrassment is the entry fee to every success. You will not get anywhere if you're not willing to put yourself out there.

Be adaptable as you venture forth in your financial life, bearing in mind that the longest-surviving creatures on earth are not the biggest or the strongest. Dinosaurs died out 65 million years ago but cockroaches have existed as a species for 300 million years and can survive almost anything. Why? Because they have the ability to adapt. They can survive without a head because they don't need a mouth or head to breathe; they don't rely on blood to carry oxygen around their bodies. Flexibility is critical in today's world because it stops you becoming obsolete. So, maintain an open mind and keep learning. Technology keeps changing and evolving – don't be like one of those grandpas who doesn't know how to unlock his iPhone! Don't be afraid of AI. Stay curious and use it to your advantage.

When making money, it's important not to chase someone else's dreams. Your mother might have pointed out your neighbour during your high school years and said, "Ah, look at him. He just made a million dollars doing X." You pricked up your ears and felt motivated, and then you signed up to study the same course the neighbour did so you could do what the neighbour was doing, even though it was not aligned with who you were and what you wanted in life. Define your core values and decide what meaningful work you want to do in the world, because there will be ups and downs along the way, and you need a powerful vision to see you through the tough times. You need a strong sense of purpose. A reason to keep going when you're lying awake at three in the morning, wondering, "Why am I doing this to myself? Why am I putting myself through all this embarrassment? Why am I showing up at all these events I don't like? Why am I doing all these difficult things? Why am I losing money?"

At this point in my life, I'm not driven by greed. I work hard for a greater purpose. If you want to be a billionaire, like I do, be a little protective of your vision. You won't necessarily be able to share it with your closest friends or family members because to some it'll sound as if you're bragging. They might say, "Really...? I'm not sure you're smart enough, financially, to be X or Y" or "But you're a woman..." Protect and nurture that beautiful vision you have.

Get inspired by the power of your imagination. If you have a thousand dollars and you donate it to an orphanage, what could you do with a million dollars? I've got a million dollars and I want to be a billionaire: what will I do with that kind of money? As a billionaire, I'll have other billionaire friends; together we can

Foundation 5: Financial

network and create something massive! How amazing it will be to spread such positivity in the world. I'm passionate about helping children, so I'll visit orphanages and give away backpacks and organise Santa Clauses at Christmas. I love that God uses my pocket to bless other people, that God gives me light and love, so I can use it to give light and love to other people. I'm just a vessel. When I'm lying awake in the early hours, as I sometimes do, I think to myself, "It's hard but it's okay. I'm divinely guided and I have all the right people in my corner, and where I'm going is the right direction."

I wish the same for you.

Journal and keep track of all five Foundations. To create your own journal, here are some guidelines on how to organise your day:

- The top section concerns your general goal for the day: **what would you like to achieve today?**
- Then, **what state of mind would you like to be in today?** Yes, you might get angry or upset at some point during the day. It doesn't matter; brush it off and keep going. Get used to these "failures" and return to your centre. Failures, from the tiny to the huge, are a part of life. Your intended state of mind for the day might be something like, "I want to be more compassionate today" because yesterday you felt angry. Or, "Today I'd like to be more focussed" because yesterday you were distracted.
- **Write down what you intend to do that day** for each of the Five Foundations. Remember, you can do as much or as little as you like. Two minutes daily for each Foundation adds up to only ten minutes of your time. Physical might entail doing star-jumps in your bedroom for two minutes

Good Girl

- or even just sitting in a chair with your feet firmly on the ground and being aware of your body. Doable, right? Listing your goals for each Foundation at the beginning of the day will take you less than a minute.
- The next section in the journal is **"What I'm grateful for today"**.
- This is followed by "**What I'm looking forward to today"**.
- On another page is the **summary**, where you get to hold yourself accountable and tick off each goal for the day.
- At night, you can also jot down what you're grateful for, in point form. You get to look at what you did that day in the Five Foundations and what you'd like to improve on the next day. It's a **quick method of keeping yourself on track**.

Download worksheets from **www.piyane.com/resources**

Good Girl
Piyané Ung

Place: _____ ☼ Date: _____

ONE thing I'd like to achieve today: _____

What am I feeling right now: _____

State of mind I'd like to be in today: _____

🌱 My physical goal today: _____

🐾 My mental & emotional goal today: _____

🪺 My community/relationship goal today: _____

🕉 My spiritual goal today: _____

🐷 My financial/skills goal today: _____

2 things I do for myself today just for me:

1. _____
2. _____

I am _____

I am _____

I am _____

Brain dump/Notes: _____

Place: _____ ☾ Date: _____

ONE thing I've achieved today: _____

What am I feeling right now: _____

_____

_____

🌱 Physical goal I've achieved today: _____

🧘 Mental & emotional goal I've achieved today: _____

💞 Community/relationship goal I've achieved today: _____

🙏 Spiritual goal I've achieved today: _____

💰 Financial/skill goal I've achieved today: _____

2 impactful ways I've added value to others today:

1. _____
2. _____

3 things I'm grateful for today:

1. _____
2. _____
3. _____

Brain dump/notes: _____

_____

_____

_____

_____

_____

_____

From good girl to bad-ass woman!

Here we are, you and me, at the end of this book. Congratulations! In a way, this marks the beginning of a beautiful journey, and that's a beautiful place to be.

We've covered a lot of ground in this book, and you might find it all a bit overwhelming, thinking, "How on earth am I going to put all of this into place to change my life?"

Rather than leave you in that kind of place, I wanted to reinforce a few final thoughts before turning things over to you.

The trap of exchanging old traps for new traps

First of all, remember: no one is the ultimate authority on things. Don't just take my values and framework on board without questioning. Don't exchange being a "good girl" for everyone else with being a good girl for your mentor or for your internalised version of this book.

You may well disagree with aspects of this book, and that's more than okay. Life is not about taking on board others' expectations (including mine), but rather tuning into what's important for *you*. Otherwise you will end up exchanging old traps for new traps.

This book is about my story and my journey. Everyone's life is different – so different people will always say different things are important. If we just follow others mindlessly, exchanging our "old" way for their "new" way, we can end up just as lost as ever.

So the bottom line is this: I want to encourage you to find your own way. Find things that bring you joy, and do more of those things.

As you unlearn old traps and behaviours, be careful not to just replace them with new traps.

What is success for you?

What does ultimate success look like for you? Not according to your parents, friends or partner; not according to any mentor or coach... and not even according to me. If your version of success looks like living in a shed in the woods, that's great! Go for it!

What is success anyway? You might look at my public profile on Instagram and think, "It's easy for you to talk about success – you have everything," But I've realised that it's not about what or how much I have materialistically, but how much I appreciate it and give myself a pat on the back for what I've achieved, that's important.

Many people would be surprised to hear that my dream of success is living in a little cottage with a chicken coop! Seeing me on Instagram in amazing outfits and visiting luxurious places might make you assume that's what I'm aiming for in life – ever-increasing luxury. But I can tell you that when I've chased after more and more things, I've ended up back on the hamster wheel and even less satisfied with what I have.

Ultimately, I want a simple life, where I wake up late and have a lazy morning, drink good coffee, maybe have a walk on the beach, and raise children in a comfortable and free environment.

How about you?

From good girl to bad-ass woman!

Focusing on what's really important

I've never heard of anyone on their death-bed, wishing they had taken on more projects or achieved more in their life. It's always the same story – people regret not having prioritised the people and relationships in their life.

Losing contact with people is an inevitable part of life. It's even more likely when you are committed to personal growth. When you change and others don't, the distance can widen between you and them, as they stay put and you move to a different place.

It's easy to become resentful when those we love don't applaud our personal growth. It can be hurtful to think that they want us to stay in a bad place, and it's sometimes challenging to respond with kindness.

It has made a difference to me when I've realised that people's resistance to me changing for the better may come from love. Yes, the love may not be the healthiest kind of love in the world, but these people "fell in love" with a particular version of me, and they want to hold onto that version of me rather than do the hard work of grief – letting go of someone they love.

If people who are important to you struggle with you changing, try to recognise the grief and loss they are feeling, and be patient and kind with them. Their responses may seem selfish, but try to feel compassion for the loss that they are experiencing. Resist the temptation to stay stuck in old patterns just to keep the relationships and dynamics familiar and comfortable – but be patient as it may take others longer to recognise the changes in you as positive.

Sometimes, however, relationships have a natural "expiry date". If those close to us prevent us from growing into a better version of ourselves, it can be important to recognise that those people may have been gifted to us just for a season. Ending a relationship does not necessarily mean that person has not been significant, nor is it necessarily a rejection of them – it can just be a natural progression through life, as we all change. It may also be important for you not to be in their lives to allow them room to grow and change.

Don't jump too high – or too low

Whilst success is desirable, we can sometimes set ourselves up to fail by placing too many things on our plate. It's impossible to always get the balance exactly right. Try not to exchange being a "good girl" for others with placing overly high expectations on yourself – this can set you on a surefire path back to anxiety and depression.

Be present in your experiences every day. Each day, focus on the purpose of what you're doing. Why are you doing it? What is it for? Thinking consciously about these things helps to avoid getting stuck in the rut of just doing something because you have taken it on board as the "right" thing to do.

Having said that, don't get stuck in a hamster wheel. Once your basic needs are in place, try aiming for higher goals. Be kind and loving to yourself and others, but also set yourself challenges to move forward. And remember – whether you are walking or crawling there, you can always move forwards.

Over to you

My mantra, learned from Tony Robbins, is "don't reinvent the wheel – model yourself on someone else who has succeeded in what you want to do."

However, in doing this, you might be tempted to follow that person to a "T" and end up losing who you are as a result. You

From good girl to bad-ass woman!

will then need to unlearn the new "you" also, just as you unlearnt the "old" you.

You may respect and look up to someone. It's okay if something they do doesn't sit right with you. Take notice of your discomfort and the ways you disagree with them, knowing that it might be right for them, but it's not necessarily right for you.

Then ask yourself, "What's important to *me*? What does the new life I am pursuing look like?" Remember, you can't get it wrong if you are following your own true sense of self.

It's okay to be overwhelmed. Don't feel you need to take on board all of what I've offered in this book; I've offered a lot of tools here, but even if you just gain one positive thing from this book, you're already in a better place.

Someone in my life, who has been an inspiration for a long time, taught me something important recently. When you're in a rut, just aim to do two things for yourself each day. For him, it's walking the dog and going to the gym – if he does those two things, he knows he's okay. For me, it's getting out of bed and getting ready for the day. Tomorrow, it might look different – maybe taking a long bath and going to the gym.

Regularly meditating on and sitting with your decisions and relationships is crucial to avoid just mindlessly adopting someone else's version of you.

What can I contribute?

By now you have hopefully started to find your true community and are thinking about your place in the wider world. Having a meaningful life is about asking, "What can I contribute?"

But here's the thing: you can contribute in different ways, from the large to the small. You don't need to be a CEO or a millionaire to make a contribution. For example, if you like to walk

Good Girl

a lot, you might have formed a community of people in your area with whom you walk every day, and that might be where you contribute your time, attention and compassion. Your story is as unique as you are.

Let's talk a bit about legacy. "What will I be remembered for? What difference will I have made to the world when I die? What is my legacy?" This forms part of the big picture of your life, and I get asked such questions a lot by those who are at the beginning of a healing journey or a spiritual path. This is one of the reasons why some people commit suicide: they don't believe they are worthy of leaving any kind of legacy.

I think we all want to make meaning out of life, but often there doesn't seem to be anything we can do that will create change in this world. We can't necessarily leave anything that will still have an impact further down the line, whether it's values, money or creative works. Our influence will probably only be seen for one or two or three generations at best, and even though others may build on what we have done in our lifetime, that's not guaranteed.

Nothing will last. The earth will probably be absorbed by the sun in about 7.5 billion years. So, if you're thinking about the scale of life itself, as a species we human beings exist in the blink of an eye. Any legacy you leave could be wiped out by a tsunami or a huge storm. In a wider sense, there is no meaning to life. The meaning of life, the legacy we leave, is what we have *today*. It's the here and now. Don't wait for that time somewhere down the track to take action; it's actually what you build now and what you do today that matters. We only have this moment. We only have what we have right here, right now.

From good girl to bad-ass woman!

Death will come, but not today... which is why today is a good day.

I believe that all of the Five Foundations are important – they've been fundamental in helping me turning my life around. But really, the first four are the primary Foundations for life. The fifth Foundation – Financial – helps support the ways we live, but the first four are about building this way of living in the first place.

So don't put the cart before the horse – don't prioritise one Foundation over the others, especially the Financial Foundation. We often end up getting stuck if we focus on the end goal of being rich or being seen in a certain way.

At the end of the day, "death and taxes" are our only certainties. As someone once said, "life is a terminal illness".

When you walk into a room, remember that everyone standing there is mortal. Take away all their positions and possessions, and you'll see human beings in front of you who will die. Rihanna, Eminem, Barack Obama – whatever big names you can think of, they will die, the same as you.

I'm hoping that by now you can hear the word "death" and not get triggered. I hope you have gained perspective and, instead of fearing death or wanting it for different reasons, you're able to think about it often, just so you appreciate that you are alive and see that your problems don't matter that much. Death will happen to me one day and I'm comforted by the thought. My time will come, but it's probably not today, so I'm going to say that today is a good day. This book contains the tools for me to be content today.

I have recovered from my depression and my suicidal ideation. These days I can talk about my experiences without tearing up because I have worked through them with the help of therapists and coaches. I am a self-love warrior! On my best days, you'll see

Good Girl

me dancing and singing; on my worst days you'll see me crying... and that's okay. We are all human and we have emotions. It's okay to have feelings. Keep showing up for yourself and you will get better, I promise you!

Your experiences and hardships transform into your sense of spiritual purpose. Depression and anxiety happened to me, but now these experiences have become part of my life purpose. I have a burning passion to host events to help others in their struggles, and this work is enormously fulfilling for me.

What are we here for? To experience love and to make our contribution. Often, we wear too many masks and lose track of who we are. We also tend to lose the joyful part of ourselves, the childlike, playful side that enjoys the moment, not weighed down by thoughts and responsibilities. We all have burdens – but we also have the ability to tap into our lightness and joy, right now. Let's get into the habit of letting go and being who we really are. To celebrate reaching the end of this book, put on some music and dance!

From good girl to bad-ass woman!

Recommended resources

Join my Facebook community: **Piyané Ung**
Follow me on Instagram: **@piyane**

Here are some recommended resources to help you on the rest of your journey:

- **BetterHelp** app is a convenient way to get professional help from a licensed therapist. The 20,000+ accredited therapists cover issues ranging from depression and anxiety to family and couples' therapy. You're matched up with a suitable professional for an affordable online therapy session.
- **Happify** app offers science-based activities and games to reduce stress, anxiety and sadness and build greater resilience.
- **Headspace** and **Calm** are my favourite meditation apps.
- **Way of Life** is a great app for habit-building. It's a habit tracker that motivates you to entrench better, healthier behaviours.

Believe that you are worthy. Believe that you are worthy of being alive. Believe that you are worthy of love *right now*, exactly as you are.

Lastly, I want to leave you with a whole lot of affirmations to use. Choose the ones that resonate with you or use them all. Say them out loud. And, go!

Good Girl

Who am I?

I am kind.
I am intelligent.
I am loved.
I am generous.
I am enthusiastic.
I am beautiful.
I am healthy.
I am passionate.
I am proactive.
I am dynamic.
I am innovative.
I am resourceful.
I am reliable.
I am confident.
I am compassionate.
I am supportive.
I am sincere.
I am brave.
I am extraordinary.
I am happy.
I am enough.

I AM WORTHY!

To Nalia,
May you always be
courageous, joyful and fearless...
knowing that you can be
whoever you want to be...
and Mommy will always
love you unconditionally.

To Ratha,
The constant strength,
The calm and steady rock,
The greatest father any daughter
could ever wish for.

www.ingramcontent.com/pod-product-compliance
Lightning Source LLC
Chambersburg PA
CBHW061735070526
44585CB00024B/2675